WHOLE FOOD PLANT-BASED DIET COOKBOOK FOR BEGINNERS

Transition to A Healthy Lifestyle and Lose Weight with Easy Recipes No Salt,
Oil, or Refined Sugar to Embrace Clean Eating | + 31-Days Meal Plan

AMY BRYLDE

TABLE OF CONTENTS

INTRODUCTION

Contrary to popular belief, whole foods and plant-based diets don't mean you can only eat fruits and vegetables. This diet is good for your body, skin, and even the environment and means that most of the food you consume comes directly from whole, unprocessed food. Some people prefer to add minimal amounts of lean meat and fish, but this book focuses on a whole-foods plant-based diet (WFPB) with no animal ingredients, no salt, no oil, and no refined sugar.

A plant-based diet can help prevent the risk of diabetes, hypertension, and heart disease (Academy of Nutrition and Dietetics, Melina V, Craig W, Levin, 2006). Starting a whole food plant-based diet has so many benefits like regulating your gastrointestinal system, helping you lose weight, and even giving you better-looking skin. All these benefits are possible when a person follows the proper diet. There are no steadfast rules that you must follow and there is no risk of failing the diet. Your health will benefit from choosing to routinely eat the right foods.

This book will explain what a whole-food diet actually is and how some slight changes to your routine might benefit your life. If most of your food consumption stems from convenience foods that come in a box and have a long shelf life, you might consider switching to a more wholesome diet. Any convenience or processed food, the opposite of what whole food is, will only fill you up but leave your body with harmful and unacceptable levels of salt, sugar, or additives.

Eating whole-plant foods requires a complete dedication to consuming only plant-sourced foods. It leaves many beginner dieters struggling as we are used to having some animal or processed foods in every meal. I have no medical expertise, but I had read and studied many books regarding the benefits of the WFPB diet before starting a WFPB diet, especially when I decided to write this book to share my experience with other people. So many positive scientific results convinced me to start my lifestyle change to a WFPB diet. I have included references and links to the specific medical-scientific research to let everyone feel free to go deeper on a particular topic.

This book aims to guide you through starting to eat healthier, step-by-step. It is not an emergency diet. It's a lifestyle change guide so that you can make better food choices daily. If once in a while you happen to "cheat" by indulging your sweet tooth or sneaking a salty snack, you should not consider yourself a failure. This diet is meant to change your life so that you can live happily, fully, and hopefully longer. This will hopefully mean leading a life with a healthy weight and fewer medications — it's a journey well worth taking.

What is fun about making meals, even a plant-based meal, is the whole process. Choosing combinations and seasoning will teach you to add a fantastic flavor and make every meal special and pleasant.

Chapter 1

THE WHOLEFOOD PLANT-BASED DIET: ORIGIN AND GUIDELINES

Considering the recent statistics, more than 10,000 people worldwide have already jumped into the whole-food diet bandwagon and are already sharing their "Life-Changing" experiences. So, of course, the first question that one might ask is the most basic one.

This diet promises to bless an individual with many physical and psychological benefits.

This systemic reset will seamlessly allow your body to reinvigorate the body's metabolic, digestive, and defensive mechanisms and, in turn, make the whole body much healthier overall.

Restrictions on diet should not be considered a factor that limits your lifestyle. Instead, you should consider that through this means you can appreciate foods that are cleaner and simpler by adjusting your food.

This journey is sure to appear difficult, but I will make sure that the guidelines you need in order to make your journey as smooth as possible are at your disposal.

The plant-based diet seems confusing because it is both described as a vegan or vegetarian diet. There are also claims suggesting that the plant-based diet should include some animal products or none.

The plant-based diet is simply a way of eating that focuses on having plant foods as a significant portion of each meal. It is a 100% plant-food style.

For this reason, one may believe that the plant-based diet is either a vegan diet (with a 100% plant-food focus) or a vegetarian diet (using some animal products). Unfortunately, both cases are incorrect, and I will tell you why.

Aside from the plant-based diet having the distinction of emphasizing plants, it strongly prohibits processed foods like bleached rice and added sugars. However, vegan and vegetarian diets allow some amounts of processed foods, which would disqualify them from being called a plant-based diet.

The choice of what ratio of plant-to-animal-to-processed foods a person eats on the plant-based diet relies on the dieter's discretion, eating habits, and health goals. For this reason, I will not make any hard and fast rules for how such proportions should be managed. My experience is that the best results come by switching entirely and exclusively to a WFPB diet with no animal ingredients, salt, or refined sugar.

The plant-based diet is not about skipping something or adding something to the menu. It is about clean eating and using the initially available stuff without forgetting the other fresh vegetables, fruits, and seeds substitutes. All you need to focus on are the naturally grown and healthy products available.

It is not hard to define what can be on your menu and what cannot. Moreover, the restrictions are evident for people shifting their diet. Another primary factor of the plant-based diet is the proper calculation of nutrition. It is a common misperception that plants do not have protein or other nutrients. However, some plants do have more protein than eggs or meat. Scientific research has proven it.

Chapter 2

THE SCIENCE BEHIND A WHOLE-FOOD, PLANT-BASED DIET

THE SCIENCE OF PLANT-BASED DIET - EATING HEALTHY

Transitioning from a meat to a plant-based diet is not as difficult as everyone thinks. You can do it gradually by increasing your fruit and vegetable intake while decreasing your meat and dairy intake. Minimizing meat consumption at first will make the transition seem effortless as you don't have to introduce drastic changes immediately.

Instead of meat and dairy, you should start consuming the following foods: fruits such as apples, bananas, and grapes; vegetables such as kale, lettuce, peppers, and corn; tubers such as potatoes, beets, and carrots; whole grains such as rice, oats, millet, whole wheat; legumes such as kidney beans, black beans, chickpeas, etc.

Therefore, you should base your diet on vegetables, fruits, legumes, whole grains, and tubers. You can start implementing these changes by replacing meat in your favorite recipes and dishes with mushrooms or beans. You will gradually lose the habit of consuming meat and switch to an entirely plant-based diet. To help your transition process, you should add more calories of legumes, whole grains, and vegetables to your everyday routine, making you feel full and thus reducing your desire to eat meat and dairy.

Before we get into the detailed, 4-week program for switching to a plant-based diet, here are a few tips to help you make the transition easier.

As soon as you start switching your diet, you will notice how positively your body reacts to receiving all the nutrients it needs to function correctly. It would be best to focus on foods like beans, legumes, berries, broccoli, cabbage, collards, nuts, and kale.

Make sure that ¾ of the plate consists of plant-based ingredients!

You can slowly transition by introducing two or three meat-free days to your week plan. As time goes by, you will get used to this system, and you will be able to skip meat more often until you finally switch to a plant-based diet.

Followers of a plant-based diet have also raved about the excellent anti-aging benefits of the diet. Collagen, produced naturally by our own bodies when we are young, is essential in making skin firm and elastic. As we age, collagen production is not as fast as before, and our skin changes, resulting in skin that is prone to sag and become thinner. Despite this being part of the natural life cycle, collagen loss can be less drastic as we get older. A plant-based diet can lead to collagen production in your body by providing all the essential nutrients and amino acids that make up collagen. If you think about it, a plant-based diet can make you feel like you've found the fountain of youth! In order to produce the amino acids that make up collagen, you should consume high amounts of fruits and vegetables like kale, broccoli, asparagus, spinach, grapefruit, oranges, and lemons – all loaded with the vital vitamin C.

The lean protein found in nuts is vital in keeping collagen around, adding to skin cell longevity and resilience. Red vegetables like tomatoes, beets, and red peppers contain lycopene, an antioxidant that protects the skin from the sun while increasing collagen production. Foods rich in zinc, such as certain seeds and whole grains, promote collagen because the mineral repairs damaged cells and reduce inflammation. So, many plant-based staples contain incredible amounts of collagen-boosting nutrients that you do not even have to go out of your way to seek.

Research shows that "people who follow a plant-based diet tend to have a lower body mass index (BMI) and are therefore leaner, healthier, and more energetic." (The American Journal of Clinical Nutrition,2009). Additionally, they tend to have lower diabetes, heart disease, and stroke rates than those who eat meat-based diets, especially processed meats.

That may be because plant-based foods such as fresh vegetables, fruits, and nuts tend to be higher in complex carbs and fiber, so they keep you feeling fuller for longer. When you're full, you're far less likely to reach for unhealthy foods that won't nourish your body or mind.

They're also high in vitamins, minerals, and antioxidants which are natural and readily absorbed by the body.

HOW A WHOLE-FOOD, PLANT-BASED DIET CAN SIGNIFICANTLY BOOST YOUR HEALTH

Scientists have proven that "many chronic diseases can be reduced, reversed, or controlled by eating whole foods and having a plant-based diet. Studies show that this diet can reduce the risk of type 2 diabetes, heart disease, certain types of cancer, and other important illnesses." (Key TJ, Appleby PN, Bradbury KE, Sweeting M, Wood A, Johansson I, 2019)

Other benefits are more significant fitness results, more energy, less inflammation, and better health outcomes after deciding to make this change.

There are many different interpretations and variations of this diet, but generally, it it does not include most, if not all, food products coming from animal or that are processed. A considerable emphasis is on eating plant-based foods that are as similar and unchanged to their original form as possible. Most followers of the plant-based diet avoid ingesting meats, dairy, as well as processed foods. There may be for several reasons behind this choice that lead us to eat or avoid particular foods.

Many people choose to be vegan because they are against the treatment farm animals go through the slaughter and poor treatment of farm animals, so they refuse to eat products that come from them. They may also opt not to wear anything of animal origin like leather or fur. Vegans will not consume even products containing traces of meat, including broths or gelatin, or products made by animals, such as honey and milk (and its derivates like cheese and butter). Other ingredients that contain animal products are more hidden, such as casein and whey. Vegans receive most of their sustenance from plant sources but not necessarily eat only products that are whole food plant-based. Some may be less health-conscious choosing to eat packaged and processed foods as well as long as they are not made of animals. So, this, technically, would not be going against their diet.

These WFPB diets may take on parameters from a vegan diet and even go beyond that by adopting whole foods in their original state. That means opting for fresh vegetables and fruit, or alternatively, frozen or dried without additives. If you eat nuts, they should be raw, while grains should not be enriched, refined or bleached.

Whatever diet someone follows, you can be sure that if they are vegan or plant-based, they will not consume any animal products unless otherwise stated.

You shouldn't hesitate to ask someone about their diet if you have questions. A few questions will actually avoid unpleasant situations of serving something they won't or cannot eat. If you are ready to listen with an open mind without any intention of judging or persuading otherwise, and they are willing to speak, you may learn a great deal!

You could assume that consuming a plant-based diet brings about many benefits. In plants you can find three types of nutrients: macro, micro, and phytonutrients. They all have different roles, but together have a positive impact on human health. For example, macronutrients allow for muscle building and provide a lot of energy, while micronutrients are active participants in a good metabolism. Phytonutrients, however, have a function in healing.

Thanks to the fact that plants offer balanced nutrition, they can help fight weight gain. In addition, fewer amounts of cholesterol can bring down high blood cholesterol levels and result in more controlled blood pressure. Therefore, those who suffer from diabetes, heart disease, high cholesterol, and obesity should all consume a plant-based, organic diet. This diet gives every individual the possibility to follow a customized diet plan for their personal health needs.

In the United States of America, dietary issues have become the primary precursor for early death. A standard American diet usually has high concentrations of saturated and unprocessed fats, including sodium and processed meat. Unfortunately, this diet has many disadvantages that will not lead to a healthier and longer life.

On the other side of the coin, a diet that seeks to promote whole foods and plant-based ingredients comes with numerous benefits. It can reduce the likelihood and exposure to risks generally associated with chronic illnesses. Thus, when you adhere to such diets, you also minimize overdependence on medication to lower the exposure to obesity and high blood pressure risks. A plant-based diet can help manage and keep some type 2 diabetes (J Geriatr Cardiol. 2017) and heart diseases (James Beckerman, MD, FACC on June 17, 2020)

A plant-based diet can benefit weight management only if you strictly follow it. However, most people who adhere to plant-based foods have reported a tremendous change in their lives regarding energy and resilience. To realize considerable success in this matter, first of all, make a shopping list of your preferences, including beans and plant-based proteins, to pave the way for other options that might lead you to live a healthy life.

You cannot achieve your targets by merely adhering to a plant-based diet. It will also require you to become attentive to the food you're eating, whether at home or out in a restaurant, simply because you have many outlets to sell unhealthy foods, supposedly plant-based items, in today's world. Such types of things would include French fries and potato chips. Therefore, constant consumption of unhealthy plant-based food can expose you to the dangers of increased weight and other chronic conditions such as heart disease.

One notable aspect of a plant-based diet that you need to be aware of — before transitioning — is that during the initial stages, you might witness some changes in your bowel movement in that you might start to be constipated or have diarrhea. The reason is that many foods on a plant-based diet have tons of fiber, making your bowel movements healthy.

Moreover, for a better transition, you need to incorporate plant-based foods gradually into your meal base to give your body enough time to respond and adjust accordingly. Finally, while in the process, be sure you maintain your fluid intake during the process itself and after transitioning.

KEY PRINCIPLES OF A PLANT-BASED DIET

- It focuses mainly on the plant, including but not limited to fruits, whole grains, vegetables, legumes, nuts, seeds, and vegetables. These should comprise the majority of the food one eats, and one should be very strict enough to follow the diet. All serving should contain more plants and less animal protein to enjoy the full benefits.
- Quality is more important than quantity; I mean fresh, locally available, or organic is healthier and nutritious. You can liaise with local farmers, get fresh farm produce, and prepare it at home. Fresh from the farm is more nutritious and very tasty. Green vegetables lose their nutrients with time if not appropriately stored; thus, you should cook them while still green.
- Always consume healthy fats and avoid refined fats and oil processed with lots of chemicals. Go for unsaturated fats, which are very good and healthy for your heart. Unhealthy fats are hard to absorb and sometimes bring health risks like blocked arteries and diabetes.
- Start your plant-based diet with breakfast because this is the meal no one would think should have any vegetables at all. You can take fruit salad, add spinach or kale to your eggs, or a cauliflower smoothie. A healthy breakfast is crucial every morning; you should take it seriously, especially starting a vegetarian diet. It will give your body the energy needed to go through the day, thus making your brain active throughout the day.
- Experiment with at least one plant every week. It will increase the variety of vegetables you're used to every week. Additionally, it will boost your nutrients every week and give you a variety to choose from, thus reducing restrictions. It will also expose you to a big world of the various plant-based meals and categorize them as easy to prepare, favorite, most nutritious, and tastier.

A plant-based, wholesome, vegan diet is healthy, even if lived and eaten this way. It consists of high-quality food, is varied, and tastes brilliant — including gluten-free, alkaline-rich products as well as fruit, vegetables, leafy wild greens, seedlings, and sprouts.

For those still eating meat because they have been used to it since early childhood, the following words may come as a surprise: A transition to a plant-based diet is effortless. Since the body stores reserves of the last meal anyway, it is not as if one would do without everything from one day to the next.

Chapter 3

HOW TO CONSCIOUSLY EMBARK ON A HEALTHY PATH

BENEFITS OF A PLANT-BASED DIET

Environmentally friendly

The plant-based diet is all environmentally friendly, so when the masses follow the plant-based diet, packaged food will be no more. So, this means that there no disposal or trash will be created. Moreover, more plants will favor more oxygen and nutrients through food. All in all, we can have a healthier and happier society.

Improved Organ Health

The plant-based diet is suitable for specific organs including the heart, liver, and kidneys. It will also improve your overall body functioning. All the organs are given proper attention so the diet will lead to a "well-oiled machine". Indeed, besides organs, the diet will allow you to get the best results by strengthening bones and increasing muscular strength, among other things. It will all depend on if and how you manage the diet because if you stick with it you will see changes within a short time.

Lowers Blood Pressure

Plant-based foods contribute to low blood pressure because they tend to have a high amount of potassium, which helps you manage your blood pressure (Physicians Committee for Responsible Medicine, n.d.). Additionally, potassium reduces anxiety and stress. Now, guess what meat has little of? That's right. Potassium. Some foods with high potassium are fruits, whole grains, nuts, and legumes. (University of Warwick,2020)

Prevents Chronic Diseases

Many medical types of research show that there are illnesses that you can avoid or minimize the risk of with a plant-based diet. The topic is vast and requires medical expertise that this book cannot cover. However, here are some official sites where you can learn more about the results of such research.

NIH National Library of Medicine https://www.ncbi.nlm.nih.gov/pmc/articles/PMC3662288/ Jaha Journal of the American Heart Association https://www.ahajournals.org/doi/10.1161/JAHA.119.012865 Academy of Nutrition and Dietetics https://www.eatright.org/

Lowers Blood Sugar Levels

One thing that plant-based diets are rich in is fiber. When you consume fiber, your body reduces the sugar it absorbs into the bloodstream. Additionally, fiber does not make you feel hungry fast. When you do not feel full, you consume more food than necessary. Plant-based foods help prevent such a situation from arising. (Appleby PN, Davey GK, Key TJ., 2002)Ideal for Weight Loss

Obesity has become a crisis in our lives today, with epidemic proportions. Many statistics reported that nearly 70% of adults in the United States are overweight or suffer from obesity. Hence, embarking on dietary measures and making lifestyle adjustments can significantly help facilitate weight loss, possibly having a positive and lasting impact on your health.

Many studies have also shown how plant-based diets are beneficial for weight loss. Due to its high fiber content, the

WFPB diet, except for processed foods, can be a winning combination for shedding those stubborn and excess pounds. (J. Geriatr Cardiol, 2017)

Consider the difference between eating heavily processed or additive-filled food directly from its source. Which one do you think will have fewer calories? Of course, it will always be the natural food eaten as it should, with no butter, oil, or fattening condiments. But unfortunately, all that processed food can cause you to gain weight maintain an unhealthy weight, and increase your risk of suffering from health issues, such as Type 2 diabetes and hypertension. If you choose to switch to a whole-food, plant-based diet you can help eliminate these risks.

Eating more while dieting sounds pretty contradictory. But it's possible! You do not have to despair if you consider a whole-foods, plant-based diet if you enjoy food. If you are looking at this process as a way to change your life, giving you a new way of eating from now on, not as a fad, you will enjoy the process and be able to eat more.

When you begin a whole-food, plant-based diet, you become more conscious about your food. Reading labels will quickly become a habit. You might be amazed at the ingredients included in your once-eaten foods. The levels of sodium, sugar, and additives that have names you cannot even pronounce could be preventing you from maintaining a healthy weight. Becoming conscious about every bite you put in your mouth can help you become the healthy weight you desire and stay that way!

When consuming a plant-based diet, you are cutting down on excess fats and maintaining a healthy weight. You won't have to be concerned with calorie restrictions! Weight loss is possible with a plant-based diet simply because of the previously mentioned fiber. In addition, it helps you manage your hunger and receive the necessary amount of minerals, proteins, and vitamins from your green meal.

Saves Time and Money

Plant-based foods are not as difficult to prepare as meat-based foods. You will take less time to schedule an organic meal. You can quickly put together some healthy ingredients and make a quick salad when needed. Furthermore, you spend less money preparing food using plant-based ingredients. When you source local and organic products, you shell out less cash for the items you would like to buy.

Lifestyle Changes

Changing to healthier foods can lead to good health and feeling better overall. Everyone should try to eliminate any bad choices, including:

- Smoking
- Drinking excessive amounts of alcohol
- Avoiding exercise
- Eating unhealthily

When you eliminate these behaviors from your lifestyle, you can focus on good behaviors and choices. Choosing foods that are not processed and are as similar to their original form as possible helps your body. Making small changes to your diet can significantly impact your overall health. Consider changes such as:

- Choosing potatoes over potato chips
- Eating apples rather than applesauce
- Adding nuts and cinnamon to your steel-cut oatmeal rather than eating instant oatmeal
- Avoid creamy sauces; choose to add fresh veggies or salsa to your dishes

Once you eliminate the "bad" foods from your diet, you can start to focus on those foods that contain good properties:

- Antioxidants — These essential vitamins help protect your cells from damage caused by free radicals. Choose from various foods, including berries, grapes, beans, and carrots.
- Phytochemicals — There are thousands of these nutrients found in plant-based foods that mimic the effects of antioxidants. Consider consuming carrots, chickpeas, broccoli, and onions to obtain these benefits.
- Polyphenols — These are nutrients known to have anti-inflammatory properties that can help protect cells against the risk of cancer, and you can find them in blueberries, raspberries, onions, and others. (Pérez-Jiménez J, Neveu V, Vos F, Scalber A.,2010)

Start with the plants you are familiar with and are locally available in your area. Then as you make it, routinely try new healthy plant-based recipes, and if you work during lunch, consider packing your lunch from home. Plant-based meals can also be used as a detox, especially when blended. It applies to fruits and vegetables that can be eaten raw.

Fruits, vegetables, and whole grains provide the fiber your body needs to cleanse itself of waste products. Seven servings each day may seem like a lot of food, but a serving of fruit is one small to medium piece or one cup, and a serving of vegetables is one-half cup.

Improved Digestion

Digestion of food is essential because it determines absorption. The plant-based meal is naturally packed with fiber, which is key to proper and better digestion. Fiber brings additional bulk to one's stool while assisting in regulating, thus smooth elimination of undigested food and stool. When absorption is adequate, the body feels functional and active, and the need is involved in various daily activities.

When digestion is proper, there is no discomfort associated with problems arising from indigestion, overeating, and eating fatty foods that stay longer in the stomach and take longer to digest and absorb. The necessary and healthy nutrients are easily absorbed in the bloodstream and comfortably removed as waste without discomfort or pain. Drinking a lot of water as recommended, also eases digestion.

Boost Energy Naturally

Plant-based meals are rich in minerals and vitamins, which give people a lot of energy. The nutrients also act as antioxidants, and the healthy protein and fats boost brain functioning and alert one. In addition, a plant-based meal is easy to digest and has that extra energy released to the body, enabling the body to be more active, boost thinking, and improve mood. It is the reason why most professional athletes love and prefer plant-based meals.

Fast foods take longer to digest, slow down metabolism, and leave the body weak and inactive, thus leading to unnecessary weight gain. On the other hand, natural energy is more effective than taking it from energy drinks since it comes due to satisfaction and not an instant boost. Thus, it is essential for everyone, not just athletes, to consume lots of plant proteins to have natural energy to carry out daily tasks.

Healthy Hair, Skin, and Nails

It's true; your hair, skin, and nails are affected by 90% of your diet. So what you feed your body and go inside your body will be reflected outside. The vitamins and minerals are suitable for the skin as they smooth it, repair dead cells, and give the skin room to breathe. Meat and dairy products can cause inflammation, which will be visible on the skin. But to achieve a smooth surface, be consistent with your plant-based diet, and be patient because the change arrives after a very long time. Skin can also appear hydrated and not dry; this is a sign of more plant-based meals in the diet.

Improved Sleep

The Whole Foods Diet goes a long way to improve and regulate the hormones in your body. It will help you improve how your body manages its internal sleep timer and improve your sleeping patterns.

Improved Focus

If you gather your nutrients from quality resources, it will make sure you have a slow and steady rate of energy during the day, leaving you feeling constantly healthy and energized.

Breaking Food Addiction

It is emotions that control the type of food you ingest more often than you think. If you feel down, you will most probably look for consolation in something sweet! If you are happy, you might treat yourself to something special, like cake!

The Whole-Food Diet should help you reason more logically so that you can choose something healthier and control your food intake.

Longevity

There is a lot of information and research supporting plant foods' potential to help us live longer. For example, suppose you put highly dense nutrients into your body and keep disease and illness at bay. In that case, it makes sense that you can live longer naturally (outside of any unexpected freak accidents, of course). So, what are the benefits of living longer? Why do we care if we have a slightly longer life? Well, there are so many reasons to strive for longevity.

Plant-based whole foods are naturally devoid of any saturated fats. The fats you find in meat, dairy, and processed foods clog your pores, cause your skin to become inflamed, and even cause acne. When you eliminate these foods from your diet, you instantly give yourself a natural facial without any procedures in a dermatologist's chair or the need for chemically filled medications. Likewise, good fruits and vegetables can provide the antioxidants and phytonutrients essential to smooth, glowing skin, and no procedures are necessary.

Better for the Environment

If we want to save our natural resources, producing plant-based foods requires much less of them. For example, compared to factory farming, it is clear that plant farming adds significantly less pollution, CO_2, and methane gases into the air. Along with fossil fuels, other precious resources, such as water and soil will have noticeably less demand.

Here are some fun facts about the costs of production on a typical American factory farm: More than 9 billion animals are raised and slaughtered yearly for human consumption.

Over 1/3 of all-natural materials and fossil fuels are used in animal production in the United States.

Approximately 7 football fields worth of land are leveled every single minute of the day to create more room for livestock and the food it takes to feed them.

The methane gases emitted by farm animals as they are digesting their food are the same kind of gas that is a contributing factor to the greenhouse effect. It has a massive impact on our environment and is a cause of global warming (a considerable imbalance and stress to the quality of our atmosphere).

- Natural stretches of land are being bought and turned into farmland worldwide. An estimated 70% of the land has been turned into farming and grazing land in the Amazon rainforest.
- Farms generate over a million tons of manure per day! It is equal to 3 times the amount of the entire U.S. population.
- Farm animal manure is stored in huge open-air lagoons and, when it leaks, it pollutes natural water sources. One such spill was recorded to have killed over 110,000 fish.
- Quite often, animals are treated with antibiotics to protect the meat and accelerate the growth or production of the livestock. Excess antibiotics are unprocessed in the animal's waste, and in large quantities, as in factory farms, this can contaminate water sources.
- More than 1,500 gallons of water is required to produce about 1 pound of beef. That is equivalent to the amount used to take 100 showers for the average American. Instead, it takes a little over 20 gallons of water to produce 1 pound of whole wheat.

The beautiful thing about our society is that we possess the technology, knowledge, and resources we need to make other choices. If we choose, we can go another route other than the meat-eater lifestyle.

GETTING STARTED

People about to enter a plant-based lifestyle are typically concerned about their protein intake. Unfortunately, as we have seen before, meat manufacturers often like to play around with the message that it is the most significant source of protein. It goes without saying that meat contains essential proteins, you can find the same proteins in plants. You have so many options to choose from that you might as well be spoiled for choice.

It's not only beneficial to your health when you transition into a plant-based menu; scientists and environmental conservatives have also found that it helps to protect your environment as well. Those who strictly observe these types of meals tend more significantly not to harm the environment in any manner.

That is because the adoption and maintenance of eating healthy plant meals help keep the emission of greenhouse gasses at a minimum. Also held in check are the factors leading to environmental degradation, such as global warming, which will also be minimal. Some studies by scientists and environmental lobbyists suggest that the most significant benefits to the environment come from eating plant-based meals and the least number of animal foods. The observations cut across various plant-based products used in vegetarian and vegan diets.

You may also notice that manufacturers say calcium is found in meat-based products. That is another myth. Plant-based food can receive all the essential nutrients — calcium included —.

Even with a plant-based diet, you can load up on all the essential micro- and macronutrients. You have numerous options to work with, allowing you to find the food that will match your nutrient requirements.

I have provided many ways that you can get into the habit of eating plant-based foods. However, if you like, you can always start with breakfast. When you start your day with plant-based foods, you prepare your mind to receive healthy meals. It is an excellent way to get used to this new lifestyle.

Focus on the things you can have, not on the ones you cannot. When you delve into all the things you are missing out on, you may find it difficult to make the change. Remember, plant-based meals are not boring. They are flavorful, colorful, and simply fun to make. You can even make a quick meal in less than 10 minutes if you are hungry and cannot wait long to eat.

Do not worry about how fast others have gotten adjusted to plant-based diets. You have to work at your own pace. Whether it means you have to sacrifice a lot of meat or eat more plant-based food, take your time to adjust to the new lifestyle.

Remember why you have adopted a plant-based lifestyle if you feel like your willpower is draining away. You have decided to make positive lifestyle changes, starting with eating right.

Another way to adopt a plant-based lifestyle is by setting goals. You feel a sense of accomplishment when you have certain goals. It also distracts you from focusing too much on what you have given up.

You will be working with dishes that cover breakfast, lunch, and dinner and enjoying snacks, desserts, and drinks. You have many ways to create the diet that you are comfortable with. Want to skip breakfast for salads? You can do that! Want to have smoothies for lunch? Sure! Dinner plus healthy desserts? You can whip up something delicious.

Beginning a diet should not be a random process; you must go through a scientific procedure and then progress. Here are some important things you need to focus on:

Know Your Body

The first thing you should bear in mind is understanding your body. Every body type is different, and not all diet plans suit everyone. A person needs to know about body reactions, needs, and conditions. Whatever we eat or consume, our body reacts to it in a specific manner. The most crucial factor is to know how your body will respond to plant-based food options. In your body type, you should focus on:

- Food allergies, intolerance, or reactions
- Nutritional deficiency in your body
- Body shape or composition
- Mood swings or hunger reactions
- Food consumption
- Set up a goal

Once you understand your body type and needs, you must move to the next step. Anything we do without any specific purpose or goal is ineffective and will take you nowhere. You need to set up a goal in the first place; that is why you are putting effort into achieving it. Starting a plant-based diet is all about being in shape, losing weight, and living smart or healthy. When you have a goal or set ambition, you can prepare yourself accordingly and follow the required steps.

Start Slow

Take a look at your food journal and determine where to start. If you notice an overabundance of snacking going on throughout your days, you can start by cutting them out. That does not mean that you need to go hungry. Swap those potato chips for cut-up green peppers for the same crunch, yet fewer calories and more taste. If you need something sweet, choose berries or apples as your snack. You can add a bit of natural nut butter to your apple for a treat. Small changes like these can get you started on a whole-foods, plant-based diet. Once you are comfortable swapping out a few snacks, you can begin to focus on your three main meals.

What Should You Have in Your Kitchen?

Regarding the plant-based diet, only one thing comes to your mind: all the food comes from plants. Therefore, you must transform your kitchen accordingly with your shift to a plant diet. It does not mean adding more plants to your kitchen garden; although that is not a bad idea. On the other hand, it is more important to exclude all the things that are not plant-based. You need to differentiate among the products and separate them accordingly.

In the next step, you can stock up on all the plant-based food products in the cabinets. Make sure not to pick up packaged products; instead, stock up on only the fresh ones. It will help you avoid any toxicity and give you all rich nutrition.

How to Prepare Your Body

You need to prepare your body before getting started with the diet plan. Everybody has reactions to diet changes and food options. You may feel issues with the food items shift if you are not a vegetarian. Therefore, you need to prepare your body before you move to make a drastic change in your food consumption. Here are some guidelines on how you can do it.

Take Small Steps

Do not start with the significant steps; instead, take some small transformation steps. For non-vegetarians, it is hard to turn toward all plant-based food options, as they do not have the resources to help them pick up the multiple choices. Therefore, they have to make small steps by incorporating some vegetables in the meal and then moving to an entirely plant-based diet.

Eliminate Allergies or Intolerance

Some people do have an intolerance to vegetable food options for multiple reasons. Remember, allergies and intolerance are two different things. Allergies lead to problematic conditions like rashes, difficulty breathing, lousy stomach, and more. Intolerance can cause psychological changes, like mood swings, no sleep, or more. It would help if you eliminated the factors that cause all these conditions from plant-based food.

Control Cravings

Several people generally cannot control the will to eat something at a specific time. It is challenging for those who love to eat everything. It is necessary to prevent these cravings in the first place so you can follow the plan properly.

Provide Substitutes

The best way to control the cravings or cheating is to have the proper substitutes for these cravings. The replacements cannot replicate the option entirely but will be able to provide you with time relief so you can have the best diet experience.

HOW TO GET THE MOST OUT OF YOUR PLANT-BASED MEAL PLAN?

Planning ahead for your meal is one of the best ways to maintain your calories and eat healthy. It can also present you with some of the best ideas to cut down on unhealthy food, prompting your family to eat healthily. It is an essential fact worth mentioning, and as much as it is true, at the same time it isn't straightforward in numerous ways. This concept, apart from being challenging, can be very tedious.

Nonetheless, we have many plant-based meal plans in this modern era, which can be very handy. These modern-day basics have made it easy for anyone keen on a healthy diet to choose what they want to eat without hassle. The right approach will thus guide you successfully when you embark on your meal planning journey. Apart from this, it enhances your creativity to a certain extent by coming up with hitherto unknown recipes to boot.

After you have achieved your healthy eating goal, you might find yourself inspiring other people on the benefits of healthy living. It will be a plus for you as you will have aligned yourself to the rigorous programs that also come with the discipline of preparing a plant-based whole meal in the long run. Practice makes perfect, and the best way to engage yourself fully in a plant-based diet is to practice how to prepare such meals consistently. In this manner, you will know the kinds of ingredients to go for on your shopping list. That will also help you develop a tangible budget when shopping for your cooking requirements. It will also make it easier for you to gradually transition into a vegan diet.

Plant-based diets will make you keep it simple and exciting as you will only have eyes for the foods that you love most. Then, when the time for shopping comes, you can choose your ingredients wisely from the grocery section at your local supermarket outlet or grocery store. In the end, you will have stocked up your kitchen shelves with some of the most delicious plant-based meals and snacks. While still learning, you must stick to simple recipes as you graduate to the more complex ones with time. With this kind of learning, you can become an expert in plant-based cooking in your home, much to the delight of your family members, friends, and extended family.

Another underlying benefit is that your delicious menu will also have the right quantities of ingredients to boot. Such a desirable experience is enough to place you at the pinnacle when successfully catering to your various needs and those of your family, especially when coming up with a weekly or monthly budget for your home. Thus, with the right diet program at your disposal, you can correctly discern the stipulated amounts of meals simultaneously, saving time by planning your meals way in advance. The correct attitude will come in handy when it comes to coming up with and implementing the right cooking style.

You are your boss here, hence at liberty to tinker with any recipe in line with your taste and preferences. You can also choose to make them old-fashioned or modern. The experience will also make you remember each step of the way, only topping up where necessary with strictly and reliable, nutritious meals. There is no better time to start your journey than now. Do not be afraid to venture into the unknown, for it is only through trying that we can succeed in our undertakings. You can also explore several avenues for more ideas, such as food blogs and magazines. You can even venture out to one of your favorite restaurants and see what they have to offer and compare it to what you are capable of. It is the best way to learn how to prepare plant-based meals.

It is up to you why you want to try a plant-based menu plan. Please do not start this diet because someone else is or do it against your will. However, you will discover when it is most likely that you have evolved into a more mature and solid state of being. Try these additional steps for success:

Write Everything Down

To avoid getting overwhelmed by events, you must write every step down as it will act as the focal point for everything regarding your plant-based meals. Jot all your reasons down and keep them somewhere where you can access them daily. It can either be a note stuck on the refrigerator door or an alert on your phone. The bottom line is to go for what works best for you. Something you can observe with much ease, something worth every time you are tempted to go back to your old ways.

Start Small but Have a Bigger Picture in Mind

It is very satisfying when you embark on fulfilling your goals of eating healthy. However, striving to maintain focus and not feel frightened by the transition prospects would be best. Take the process in your stride and stroll through it, no matter how hard, one day at a time, and you will succeed before you realize it. While some people won't find any hurdles when transitioning, many will find it overwhelming.

Eat One Meal a Day that is Plant-Based for 11 Days Consecutively

Even though it seems impossible, you can achieve it. You can try eating one plant-based meal daily for about 11 days and then gauge if there is any significant change in your health. You might end up losing some considerable weight. However, you will also feel more energetic, sleep better, and have easy bowel movements. Plant-based meals will also help your body fight many diseases, which might slow you down.

Drink Water in Place of Sugary Drinks

You can drink water instead of soda or any other sugary drinks. It is because, with water, it is very easy to tone down on those calories you do not need in your diet. According to experts, you do not have to drink water alone. You can include a variety of fruits in your diet as well. Vegetables also contain much water necessary for bodily functions, keeping you full and hydrated simultaneously. Meals such as strawberries and eggplant have approximately 90–99% water, another option to keep your body healthy and hydrated.

Fully Transition

Getting rid of meat is the first step in fully transitioning to a plant-based diet. But there are other things you still need to do. Remember, your goal is to transition fully to the recommended plant-based diet as soon as possible. It will give your body enough time to adjust to the diet, and you'll be able to see the benefits of sticking to the diet. As such, you need to get rid of eggs and dairy. Many people think that giving up dairy is the one thing that can stop them from embracing a plant-based diet. But it can be done. Think about it. Less than 40% of adults can digest lactose. If you can't digest lactose, you'll face issues such as flatulence, bloating, diarrhea, cramping, and nausea. The sugars you consume will get stuck in the colon and begin to ferment. As such, you have added a reason to stop consuming dairy.

Another thing you need to stop eating is eggs. Yes, this includes the eggs you use in baking. Instead of using eggs, you can use things such as flax eggs, bananas, and chia eggs.

Rethink How You Shop

Now that you've gotten rid of meat, eggs, and dairy, it is time to rethink how you shop. Start by clearing out your pantry. Get rid of any food product you should not consume in the plant-based diet. Next, consider what you need to purchase and where you'll likely get it. Instead of browsing the supermarket aisles, you may need to change tactics and head to the farmer's markets and farms whenever possible. This way, you'll get fresh produce at lower prices. Don't waste time on things you can no longer eat. Avoid such sections if you can. A list of what you need will come in handy.

It would help if you also familiarize yourself with the practice of checking labels. Remember, you are now on a plant-based diet. Therefore, animal products should not have a place on your shopping list. Reading labels will help you see any red flags, and as such, you'll be able to avoid such products.

A QUICK FOOD GUIDE

Most people believe that among the most challenging tasks concerning preparing a meal is how to come up with the correct quantities for eating. It is true, especially for those who want to eat healthily by preparing meals. Hence, it is imperative for people to generally watch what they eat to keep their weight in check, otherwise leading to many complications in the future. And concerning this, any meal preparation requires different recipes and portions to prepare. Therefore, it is imperative to prepare these meals for family members to benefit from all their nutritional needs. That is why you must consider the right quantities before cooking and serving you and your family members. Having this in mind, you can now fix the right amount to prepare and what time you are supposed to eat this meal. Anyone needs to be conscious of their weight. Plant-based meals will also enable you to strictly follow the guidelines for healthy eating and making recipes for such meals. A sensible plant-based meal plan will also ensure that you place clear boundaries and targets when cooking.

The key to successfully transitioning to a WFPB diet is making sure you carefully plan and prepare ahead of time, much like the vegan diet. If your diet is healthy for you, you will need to consume the foods that will provide you with the types and amounts of nutrition required for living a healthy life. For example, you don't think twice about certain nutrients when your diet includes meat and dairy; however, if you no longer consume these kinds of products you will need to find different sources to reach the appropriate level of nutrition to ensure overall wellbeing.

Increase greens in your diet. Various vegetables are present, choosing to offer different flavors and textures for soothing your tongue. Pick vegetables regularly for meal bases and as a substitute for snacks that aren't healthy for you. The crunchiness and taste of some vegetables could make it less likely to eat junk food.

Most healthy diets don't just forbid the consumption of fats but instead tell you to replace bad fats derived from animals with good ones derived from plants. Olive oil as well as seeds are good sources of healthy fats that do not negatively affect our cholesterol levels.

Cut down on meat, especially red meat, as much as you can. You can still eat it if your diet is more lenient, but it is not encouraged. Replace your meat with seafood or tofu, which can be a good substitute.

Rather than putting desserts on the table, you should place fruits or fruit dishes. They can satisfy your sweet tooth while being a healthier option. Some people crave sugar more; they can slowly cut out sugar from their diet by switching to sweet fruits instead.

Replace everyday cow's milk with soy, almond, rice, or coconut for plant-derived milk.

Stay away from foods with a lot of sugar like soft drinks or high in fat like french fries. Also, do not buy processed food because they are riddled with salt and sugar, which are enemies to your body.

Be aware that not every nutrient is provided fully and arrange a replacement. Vit B12 is present in some cereals and nutritional yeast. Iron is also less consumed, so eat a healthy dose of cabbage, spinach, or kidney beans to make up for it.

Get Your Phytochemicals

How do you fill your diet with these amazing nutrients? Start by creating a rainbow of colors on your plates. The more colorful fruits and vegetables you consume, the higher the chances of consuming the nutrients your body needs. There are many beautiful colored fruits and vegetables to choose from, such as blue blueberries, pink watermelon and grapefruit, green kale and spinach, orange carrots, as well as red tomatoes, strawberries and raspberries.

Does It Need to Be Organic?

Just because you want to try to eat whole foods it does not mean that they must buy only locally grown or organic products. Likewise, don't think that whole foods shouldn't be organic. Let's just say that to qualify as whole or natural it is simply not necessary to be organic. Organic food can have the added advantage of not containing harmful chemicals, which is another factor that can contribute to choosing to eat whole foods.

Maximize the Amount of Nutrients in Vegetables

Apart from what is mentioned above, we will also be eating tasty food to get the nutrients that are vital for our good health. When you consume food that has been modified, processed, or refined, the important nutrients are removed. It is even true for those foods that you consider healthy. For example, you might think you are doing your body good by eating spinach or broccoli. But if you do not eat it raw or prepare it properly, you will likely lose some of its nutrients, especially water-soluble ones. Vitamins B and C are two vitamins that are water-soluble and that can be consumed in vegetables that, however, are lost when cooked in water, both if steamed or boiled. Therefore, raw vegetables are the best way to consume all vital nutrients. If you prefer cooked vegetables, you can choose among "quick-cooking" methods such as stir-frying, sautéing or blanching to avoid the risk of losing too many nutrients.

Choosing Whole Grains

In addition to eating fruits and vegetables, a whole-food diet includes eating various whole grains. Be careful when you choose which grains you eat, however. Not all whole grains are as "whole" as they are made out to be. If you choose the right type of grains, you are enhancing the taste, texture, while adding proper nutrition to your diet and reaping the benefits of complex carbohydrates and vital vitamins and nutrients.

Our grains come from the seeds of various types of grass. Grains include rice, barley, oats, cornmeal, and, of course, wheat. Grains in their original state are considered whole, with their most vital ingredients – bran and germ – not lost while processing, along with their fundamental nutrients. Processing leads to refined and, often, enriched grains, so that products such as white bread and white rice can have a longer shelf life. Any foods that have the words "refined" or "enriched" aren't healthy for you so you should steer clear. In refined grains, you can never replace lost nutrients. Enriched grains are products fortified with nutrients without providing the same benefits of the natural nutrients you get when eating whole foods.

Don't Neglect Your Iron Intake

This is another nutrient that is easily found chicken and red meat, which are staples in the Western diet. Iron is available in plant sources like leafy greens, legumes, and beans, but the body does not as easily absorb the iron from those sources as the iron content coming from meat. In order to absorb more iron from plant-based foods, you should pair a plant food rich in iron with a food that is rich in Vitamin C (citrus fruit is a great example). Adding some slices of mandarin oranges to a salad of leafy greens is a tasty and healthy way to do this. Remember that the absorption of dietary iron is inhibited by calcium, so make sure to keep the calcium-rich foods away from this combination.

EAT MORE WHOLE GRAINS THAT WILL KEEP YOU FULL AND FIT

If you change your refined grain foods like white bread and white pasta for more whole grains, you will add fiber, iron, and B vitamins to your daily diet.

It's a new challenge but it's not so complicated to adopt a more plant-based diet or even fully convert to a vegan diet. Only you can determine what goal you want to reach. Will you just be adopting more of a plant-based diet or will you go for a full-on vegan lifestyle? It's up to you. Remember that when trying new foods, do so with an open mind but with caution. Do not buy a large amount of vegetables you don't like the taste of because you will never eat them. Do not be afraid to experiment, but begin with those vegetables, fruits, whole grains, seeds, and nuts you already know you like and build meals around those items. Then start adding in new food items. You will be surprised at the endless variety available in your food choices.

Add In Some Flavor

You do not have to miss out on some healthy condiments. You can choose from options such as salsa, pesto, tahini, hummus, guacamole, and sauerkraut, to name a few. You can always get quinoa or teff flour when you want a few replacements for white flour.

Stock up on whole-grain foods whenever you notice a sale at your local store. This way, you save more and do not have to spend on individual products.

Always make sure that you have your basic baking items with you. Apart from choosing the right flour, it would help if you ideally had baking soda and baking powder (yes, both are necessary).

Snack Ideas

Many people have the most difficulty switching their snacks to a whole-foods, plant-based diet. Considering all of the available convenience foods, try to convince yourself to go that extra step and eat whole foods. Rather than succumbing to preservative and additive-laden snacks, take these few simple steps:

At the beginning of the week, chop up plenty of fresh fruits and vegetables and portion them into individual bags. Then, when you want a snack, you can grab a bag and go — it's the same as prepackaged food!

Buy In Bulk Whenever Possible

It allows you to try new whole grains, nuts, and seeds and also will enable you to make up your mixes. Don't buy pre-packaged trail mix; create your own. Add grains, seeds, nuts, raisins, and dates for a genuinely excellent and wholesome snack.

Don't Get Bored

Use hummus, nut butter, and salsa to your advantage. Dip your veggies and fruits in them for a little more flavor.

Keep whole-grain tortillas and bread on hand. During those downtimes, they can fill you up and reduce the risk of grabbing that unhealthy candy bar or other sugar-laden snacks.

Eliminate Eggs from Your Diet

Next, eliminate eggs from your diet. Usually, most people cannot eat many eggs without their bodies complaining. Therefore, it is easier to give up eggs. However, it would be best to be careful about foods that use eggs as ingredients. Yes, it would help if you gave up those cakes and pasta. However, you can do the transition slowly — it doesn't have to happen over 24 hours.

Stop Using Dairy

Dairy is one thing that many people have a difficult time giving up. They eat cheese and enjoy things like yogurt and ice cream. Nevertheless, you can successfully cut it out from your diet. An excellent way to do this is to find foods you can eat in place of dairy. When you find a suitable alternative, you'll soon be able to let go of dairy.

Start Consuming Whole, Unprocessed Foods

The final step is to switch to whole, unprocessed foods. It means you need to step up your shopping game. You have to start looking for whole foods consciously. Make sure you read and pay attention to labels when you do your shopping. In addition, stock up your kitchen with foods that are good for you to make following a plant-based diet easy.

Always keep in mind that not all foods are created equal. It's up to you to make a choice that will allow you to reverse disease, heal sickness, feel great and lose weight!

PREPPING YOUR PLANT-BASED KITCHEN

I want you to consider your kitchen your strongest ally on the road to greater health. Are you inspired? Feel free to switch up the décor in your kitchen to make it more meaningful and to make it more conducive to preparing and eating healthy meals. You want to feel inspired and in control of yourself when you walk into the kitchen to create a meal or grab a snack. If you don't have everything you need to experience, you can slowly plan to acquire these items over time gradually; and improvise the rest. While transitioning to vegetable proteins, check out the many types of mock meats or textured vegetable proteins available.

Everything else can go. It may be more enjoyable to enlist a helper for this job, or you may want to tackle it all yourself like a nutritional warrior. Either way, we are going to separate the good from the ugly. I like to start in the pantry and cupboards, pull every single item out, put it on the table or counter, and begin sorting objectively. First, you can separate the food you eliminate into 3 categories — toss, pass on and donate. Next, you can give any items you think a friend or family member will use (this can also be nice when an item is open but still good). Finally, you can donate unclaimed food still in good condition to a local shelter or food bank.

Here are a few things to consider:

Create a Good Environment

A kitchen is where you will spend a lot of time; hence, it should be pleasing to your sight and personality.

Look up a few dream kitchen ideas and use this opportunity to create that kitchen that sparks joy. Paint the walls with bright colors, hang up some fun pictures and inspirational quotes, stick recipes you want to try on magnetic boards, and give your cupboard a reorganization.

You can also consider growing herbs indoors by your windows; these are excellent for creating an inviting fragrance in the kitchen.

I like to listen to music while I cook, so I keep a good speaker nearby where I can put my favorite cooking music playlists. Dream big and make your kitchen your special sanctuary!

Be Organized

A disorganized kitchen will kill your plant-based mood.

Find ways to hide pots, pans, plates, cups, etc., in your cabinet, and if you do not have enough cabinet space, you can install hangers to organize these appropriately.

Also, it is a good idea to invest in storage jars for spices, nuts, seeds, whole-wheat flours, rice, pasta, etc. Additionally, I like to label my jars so that I can find them easily and increase orderliness.

I also love to use cutlery dividers and plate racks to keep things out of my way as much as possible. I implore you to compromise on any opportunity to keep your kitchen organized. It greatly impacts your willingness and enthusiasm for cooking healthy food.

Stock Up with the Right Stuff

Now that you know what foods you can indulge in, head out and go grocery shopping.

Following a meal plan and creating a shopping list that fits your plan is advisable. This list will serve as a guide for shopping to prevent unwanted purchases.

In return, immediately segment your groceries into the various kitchen where they belong.

- Fresh and frozen foods for the refrigerator
- Dried ingredients, oils, seasonings, condiments for the jars and pantry, etc. Remember that the goal is always to be organized before, during, and after grocery shopping.

TOOLS AND UTENSILS

When they start the plant-based diet, some people purchase new pots, saucepans, cutlery, knives, etc., as they don't want utensils that had previously been used for animal foods.

I don't think it is necessary, especially if you do not have the budget. Instead, please thoroughly clean your current utensils and wash off any residues of animal foods that are stuck to them. After doing this, things should be as good as new.

Meanwhile, you can scan through the recipes, make a list of utensils you currently don't own, and purchase them for easy cooking.

Here is also a list of utensils and gadgets that are a must-have when starting the diet.

Glass Storage Containers

Glass storage containers are fantastic for meal prepping. They retain food flavor well and are see-through for easy identification and portable for proper organization.

I also like those good-quality glass containers that are easy to clean and do not keep food flavors trapped in them after washing. Unlike some plastic storage containers that may be stained from foods and retain food odor for long, glass containers are the opposite.

Mandolin

These tools are great for slicing, spiralizing, cutting, and trimming vegetables into shapes that make your foods look inviting and interesting. Since this diet is plant foods focused, making good use of your ingredients in appetizing shapes is a great thing to do.

Pressure cooker

It is expensive, but it is an excellent choice for cooking foods quickly and pressure-cooking hard ingredients like beans. Plant-Based dieters may want to invest in one quick and delicious cooking!

Tofu Press

Pressing tofu can be messy and takes time — many don't have the patience. Using a tofu press makes the work easier so you can enjoy your tofu dishes.

Grater and Microplane

It is great for shredding vegetables and plant-based cheeses.

Air Fryer

An air fryer may also be expensive, but since the plant-based diet seeks not to include deep-fried foods, the air fryer can scratch that itch for fried food while being a healthier option.

Steamer Basket

A steamer basket is great for softening vegetables while preventing them from losing their nutrients in the boiling water used during steaming.

Lemon Squeezer

Many plant-based recipes use lemon juice so a lemon squeezer may be an essential tool.

High-Speed Blender, Food Processor, and Immersion Blender

All these tools are excellent for blending many ingredients into different levels of smoothness. They are helpful for soups, smoothies, batter, or dough prepping. You will need at least one of these in your kitchen for sure.

Baking essentials

Make your way to the cake store and buy some cake pans, electric mixers, loaf pans, muffin trays, baking sheets, etc., for the many baked foods that await your exploration.

Colander

When you need to drain those vegetables and pasta, a colander is a right tool. It becomes particularly useful when you have to divide pasta from hot water.

Parchment Paper

Since there is quite a little baking, I recommend having parchment paper. It is a grease-proof paper that allows you to bake without holding on to any grease. It will be perfect when you do not want the food sticking to any surface inside the oven.

Cutting Board

A cutting board is essential for almost every kitchen. Get two if you typically keep your chopped veggies on the cutting board, giving you more space to work with.

Measuring Cups

If you want to get accurate measurements for certain liquids, these cups will help you with that.

Scissors

It is an underrated tool that helps you cut pasta or a lot of packets and containers.

Whisk

You might have seen them used especially for eggs, but the tool can be used to mix numerous ingredients.

Blender/Food Processor

It is important to have a good blender or food processor on time when saving time. With an excellent blender with sharp blades, you can make anything from smoothies to soups to ice cream with little to no effort. A food processor isa little less necessary, but they are great to have on your hands when working with seeds and nuts.

Silicone Baking Mat or Parchment Paper

Speaking of saving time, who enjoys cleaning the dishes after working so hard on the cooking portion of the meal? To help keep cooking clean and quick, you'll want to invest in silicone baking mats or parchment paper. It will save at leastone dish from having to be cleaned!

Knives

I cannot express how important sharp knives are in cooking. As you incorporate more fresh produce into your plant-based diet, you can expect to do a lot of chopping, mincing, and dicing. When you have dull knives, there is nothing more frustrating than trying to chop through hard vegetables and being unable to. I suggest having one big knife to do most of your chopping, but it is always good to have a few medium knives on hand for smaller slicing.

Proper Storage Containers

Last but not least, the key to successful meal prep is proper storage containers. This way, you do the cooking, place them into their container, and then all you have to do is grab and go! It saves you time, space and stops you from wasting food! It is a win-win situation!

Sauté Pan

Sauté pans that are high-walled, like woks, should also be in your kitchen.

Measuring Cups and Spoons

Keep a set of measuring cups and spoons, as well as larger-sized glass measuring cups.

Strainer

A strainer allows you to drain water or broth from boiled vegetables, but it can also be used as a steamer rack in a large-sized stockpot.

Baking Sheet

Baking sheets that will be required for roasting vegetables or vegetables meats.

Thermometer

A good quality thermometer will allow you to cook correctly.

Julienne Peeler

It will help you create amazing vegetable noodles that add a hefty dose of variety to your Julienne Peeler.

Zester

A zester will create tiny pieces of orange or lemon peels for your meal for the recipes that might require it.

Citrus Juicer

It will allow you to squeeze lemon and lime easily.

STOCKING YOUR PANTRY

You should make it a habit to stock your pantry with the types of food you want to eat, as they say, out of sight, out of mind. If you want to add certain foods to your diet, you need to be able to reach for them whenever you need them. Staples such as vegetables and fruits should always be in your pantry along with legumes, nuts, whole grains, healthy fats and seeds. It would certainly help to have a few recipes nearby to plan what you'll need to buy.

Don't go overboard when you are shopping. You don't need to stock your pantry with foods you won't eat. Instead, it would be wiser to find a few foods you intend to use frequently and ensure you have enough of them. For example, you can shop bulk for things such as rice and oats and decide to shop weekly for fresh fruits and vegetables. Then, as time goes by, you'll have a good idea of how much food you'll eat, and your shopping will become easier.

What to expect: after 20 days, you should have fully transitioned to the plant-based diet in the first two weeks. After 20 days, you can check your progress to see if you are on the right track. You will notice certain things after 20 days on the plant-based diet.

Once you fully switch to the plant-based diet, you should expect to have bad days. Yes, some days will be more difficult than others. It is especially so in the first few days of fully transitioning. You will crave certain foods. You will desire animal products and start 'dreaming about' foods you can no longer eat. It is normal. But as days go by, the cravings will subside. Something else that you'll notice is that your taste buds will be much stronger. The various foods you'll be eating will contribute to a boost in taste and sensation. You need to give yourself time to adjust before determining whether or not you like a particular type of food.

On a positive note, you'll soon notice that you have a lot of energy. This energy will be consistent throughout the day. It won't fluctuate. Things like afternoon' slumps' will be things of the past. If you were used to sleeping during the day, you'd find that you are more alert throughout the day. As such, your days will become more productive. If you take advantage of this, you'll be able to experience improved sleep during the night.

Once you give up eggs and dairy, you'll notice a change in how you feel. If your body is constantly experiencing aches and pains, you'll find relief. It is because the foods you'll be eating will be full of anti-inflammatory properties. They will help you get rid of chronic pain.

As you fully embrace the diet, you may find yourself fielding questions from your friends and family. People will be curious, and some will be suspicious as they see your changes. They will have questions, and some may discourage and make fun of you. However, it should not stop you from completing the program. It is the time to remind yourself of your motivations, and while you're on it, you need to learn to upgrade your diet.

Want to know what you can eat and what to stay away from? What can you indulge in now and then? Stock up on essentials and never buy what you don't need.

When you start eating whole low-carb foods, there will be less food in your pantry since you will buy fewer processed foods. You will shop the store's outer perimeters for fresh fruits and vegetables, fish and meat, cheese and milk. Avoid the inner aisles that stock all processed foods.

You might wonder if it will cost more to eat low carb, but it is cheaper. This is because you won't be buying chocolate, sweet treats, sugar, flour, rolls, wraps, bread, and junk food. Instead, utilize the store's specials to find fruits and vegetables on sale. You might also find specials on meats.

You will spend more money on superior quality ingredients, but you will be shopping less. Anything you spend is an investment in your family and their health.

You will also be saving money on taking out food. One night's take-out meal could easily add to the same as feeding a family for a few days on healthy food.

Check labels for fat and carb content, as distinct brands can vary. Read every label on all the products you buy. It can be a revelation. You will learn what safe brands to buy and what to stay away from. For example, tuna might be packed with wheat and sugar; others are packed in olive oil.

Healthy foods can have sugars added to them. When figuring out recipes, make sure you have picked the correct brand of food that you are using since nutritional values could vary. Then, just subtract the fiber from the total carb value to figure out net carbs.

Below you will find a shopping list:

Sauces and Flavorings

- Vinegar
- Fresh herbs

- Spices and herbs

Pantry Ingredients
- Almond meal and flour
- Sugar-free jelly
- Coconut shredded, unsweetened
- Cocoa
- Stevia, erythritol
- Coconut flour
- Ground almonds
- Nuts and seeds
- Canned tomatoes
- Olives, stuffed or black

Fats and Oils

Stay away from seed oils like omega 6, canola, and sunflower. Use the following oils:

- Macadamia oil
- Coconut oil
- Avocado oil

INGREDIENTS FOR SALADS
- Fruits
- Vegetables except for root vegetables like potatoes, parsnips, carrots, etc.

GETTING PREPARED

Before starting a whole food plant-based diet, determine how you will prepare your meals. The more prepared you are, the more likely you will make this a permanent lifestyle change. Consider your various cooking methods, including:

- Grilling
- Sautéing
- No-Cook Meals
- Cooking Grains

Grains are not as time-consuming as they sound. All you need to do is boil water, add in the grain of your choices, such as quinoa or brown rice, and simmer until the liquid has disappeared! Now you have a good basis for a beautiful plate filled with whole grains topped with delicious vegetables and any spices you wish to add.

Cooking Beans

Beans require a little more work, which is why it is beneficial to do this preparation once a week to save time. First, lay them out before you soak your beans to locate the bad ones. It also allows you to remove any other particles that might have made their way there. The next step involves soaking them.

You can do it overnight way or the quick way:

OVERNIGHT

Cover the beans with 3 inches of cold water and cover them. They will need to sit for at least 8 hours, which is why it is the overnight method.

QUICK METHOD

If you are in a hurry, you can cover the beans in a pot with the same amount of water. Bring the water to a boil and leave it for 1 minute. Then, remove the beans from the heat, cover them and have them sit for an hour.

After draining your soaked beans, you will cover them with 2 inches of water and add any spices or onion you want to add for flavor. Next, bring the water to a boil and let them simmer, covered for the next 1 to 1½ hours.

Fast Meals

Every family is busy and runs into those days when no one has time to sit at the table and eat a meal. Don't resort to convenience foods during these times. Be prepared with foods already made in the freezer, such as:

- Bean burritos made with whole-grain tortillas
- Potatoes with a few spices can make a quick meal
- Sweet potatoes provide even more nutrition
- Find your favorite recipe for veggie burgers and make them in bulk to have on hand in the freezer
- A handful of fruits and nuts are always a good way to fill up on healthy food
- Soup can also be made in bulk and stocked full of veggies. Freeze the leftovers for a quick meal.

Eating a whole-food, plant-based diet requires a little dedication and the desire to want to live a long, happy life. Whether you adopt one of the techniques discussed in the book or all of them, any change is good for your health. Take it slow as you figure out what you and your family like, and then you can successfully transition to a whole-food, plant-based diet!

Pantry Stocking Tips

1. Protect your whole grains from bugs or mold. The best way to do this is by locking them in airtight containers.
2. Stock up on canned beans because they add more content to the food you are preparing; however, make sure you are not picking any high-sodium or salt beans. The labels will help you decide on what you are looking for. Make sure that you are aware of the other ingredients as well.
3. If you love cereals, don't remove them entirely. Simply pick the ones that are low on sugar and have whole-grain ingredients. That way, you enjoy breakfast (although some lip-smacking recipes might just make you forget). What about oats, you say? You can find whole-grain and gluten-free oats in the market that will fit your purposes. One can say that they are pretty outlandish!
4. Throw in a couple of your favorite hot sauces if you like to heat things. A little spice is not going to bite. Or maybe it does.

LEARNING TO READ LABELS

Adopting a new eating style and becoming more aware of what is coming into your body can be a pretty overwhelming endeavor. But with the right knowledge and a lot of practice, you will be able to find out what is in anything you are eating, and you will be able to decide for yourself if it is something you will choose to eat. So, the first step to improving something is awareness.

For many people, the nutritional facts on food mean very little when making food choices. For one, it can be a challenge to understand precisely how nutritional information correlates to what is going on in your body. I think the number of calories is probably at the most basic level of understanding how to use food labels. Your body requires a certain number of calories per day to maintain your weight and current level of nutrition. Your body uses a specific range of calories daily by being alive and moving around. The more physically active you are, the more calories are burned. The more calorie-filled foods you eat, the more calories are stored in your body, usually as fat. Having more muscle in your body means that you can burn more fat.

Food manufacturers will try everything to get their products in the shopping cart of potential customers. There are quite a few tricks that they employ to make the items seem like they are more than they really are. Here are some things you should watch out for when shopping for healthy products.

- When something has the tag "Natural," it does not mean it has natural ingredients. Even the U.S. Food and Drug Administration (FDA) cannot conclude how best to define the term. Hence, when using that word, manufacturers can pack the product with extra ingredients, such as sugar.
- There is a difference between 100% whole grain and multigrain. Do not go for the latter because some grains may not be whole.
- When something says, "No Added Sugar," it is true to an extent. You see, you need to be aware of the various forms of artificial sweeteners in the market. Check the label to see if you notice ingredients such as sucralose or aspartame. In other cases, the products labeled with "No Added Sugar" may not have added sugars, but it does not mean that some have natural sugar content. Always check for "Sugar-Free" products and look at the ingredients to ensure they do not have any sugars.
- If you notice a product that says "50% less fat," then it does not mean anything. Think about it this way: just because half has reduced the fat does not mean that there still isn't a lot of fat. That's because the "50% less" tag is an arbitrary percentage, and it is not compared with anything else.

SOURCING VITAL NUTRIENTS ON THE WFPB

While the plant-based lifestyle comes with numerous benefits, not focusing on deriving other essential nutrients that are mostly found in animal foods can be harmful to your health. Instead, source these nutrients from the following:

Vitamin B-12

Like iron, vitamin B-12 is essential for optimal brain functioning. Additionally, it helps in the production of red blood cells. Vitamin B-12 is not found in plant foods naturally. However, it can easily be obtained in meat. Since you are switching sides, knowing where you can get this nutrient is imperative.

The absence of vitamin B-12 in plant foods shouldn't discourage you from strictly avoiding animal-based products. Instead, you should consider taking vegan supplements to provide this nutrient. If you do this, ensure that you discuss this with your physician and recommend the best supplements.

However, even scientific research is not so clear on this topic. Some researchers say that B12 is only available from animal sources, and others that it is possible to find this vitamin in fortified foods, including cereals, nutritional yeast, hemp milk, and meat substitutes. (Tucker KL, Rich S, Rosenberg I, Jacques P, Dallal G, Wilson PW, et al.,2000). Before purchasing these products from the stores, you must read the nutrition labels. This way, you avoid taking home foods high in sugar and other unhealthy oils.

Vitamin B-12 is a crucial nutrient for cell and blood health. If you have a deficiency in this nutrient, you could have anemia as well as nerve damage. (https://www.nhs.uk/conditions/vitamin-b12-or-folate-deficiency-anaemia/)

Therefore, dieters can consider taking B-12 supplements or eating foods like plant-based milk, whole-wheat cereals, and nutritional yeast. (Michael Greger M.D. FACLM · February 8, 2012)

Omega-3 Fatty Acids

Omega-3 fatty acids reduce inflammation, memory, and other chronic conditions. However, they are highly sourced from fish, seafood, and other animal sources.

To derive your fair share of this nutrient from plant foods, consume hemp seeds, walnuts, and flaxseeds. However, at digestion, the body derives omega-3 ALA, which the body finds slow to convert to EPA and DHA, the two primary omega-3 fatty acids that the body can use immediately. Thanks to Omega 3 fatty acids you can lower the risk of heart diseases and improve the immune system. Fatty fish and other seafood are the best sources of this nutrient. Omega 3 fatty acids can be obtained through various plant sources, including chia seeds, organic canola oil, flaxseeds, and flaxseed oil.

Therefore, for WFPB dieters, it is essential to substitute with plant-based omega-3 fatty acids supplements. "Foods that are good sources of n-3 fats should be emphasized. They include ground flax seeds, flax oil, walnuts, and canola oil" (Davis BC, Kris-Etherton PM, 2003)

Omega-3 fatty acids are also essential nutrients that the body cannot produce. Omega-3 fatty acids come in three forms (Harvard T.H. CHAN,2022):

* Docosahexaenoic acid (DHA)
* Alpha-linolenic acid (ALA)
* Eicosatetraenoic acid (EPA)

People who regularly consume fish usually get the much needed DHA and EPA. ALA, instead, can be found in plant foods. Luckily, the body has the ability to convert ALA obtained from plants into DHA and EPA. However, the process is not as efficient. Consequently, you could supplement your diet with hemp seed oil, flaxseed oil, or chia seeds to optimize the conversion process.

Other recommended foods to include are algal oil, walnuts, perilla oil, and Brussels sprouts.

The information outlined here should help you understand that those important nutrients we often believe to be found only in animal products will also be present in some plant foods. Consequently, it is important to know what nutrients you can get from your plant foods. Only in this way can you confirm that you are obtaining all the vital nutrients to optimize your body's functioning.

Vitamin D

Vitamin D is necessary for a healthy immune system, bones, and muscles. Plant sources of vitamin D are almond milk and some cereals.

It is found naturally in foods such as fatty fish, beef liver, egg yolks, and cheese. These foods are not part of a vegan diet, so you might need to look to other sources for your daily requirement of Vitamin D. Eating soy products, drinking fortified orange juice, or "just spending 10 to 15 minutes in the sun a day will give you the vitamin D your body needs". (Amanda Barrell, 2021)

Make sure you get your vitamins from your food when it is possible.

Since the typical Western diet provides you with Vitamin D from milk, yogurt, and fish, it is often overlooked. On a more plant-based diet, you will need to spend some time in the sun every day, about 10 minutes, or drink fortified non-dairy drinks such as orange juice, almond milk, or soy milk. The Western diet also allows you to get your amounts of Vitamin B-12 from dairy foods, eggs, poultry, fish, and meat. On a plant-based diet, it might be necessary to take a supplement. Vitamin B-12 can also be found in fortified energy bars and cereals.

Fat

Fat is used immediately in the presence of physical activity, or it will be stored as fat in the body. Fat is stored up if we are ever faced with a food shortage and need to be protected against starvation. Unless you have a specific life complication where you go hungry often, we do not have a food shortage in most developed countries. We have a surplus of calorie-dense food that lacks any nutrition. This is where much of our excess fat comes from.

But all fats are not created equal. Our bodies really need fat to be healthy, lustrous, and feel satisfied with our meals. You want your diet to have plenty of good fats to keep the right balance. Healthy fats are unrefined and come mostly from plants, nuts, and seeds. Things like avocados and coconut oil provide wonderful healthy fats. So, nuts and seeds like flax and chia. Snack on plenty of nuts and seeds!

Carbohydrates

This is essentially for your physical energy.

The first 5 ingredients make up most of that food and contain about 95% of the whole when it comes to the ingredients list. After that, all ingredients descend in order of concentration. Look out for chemical-laden ingredients which are hard to pronounce and sound unfamiliar or not descriptive of what it is originally derived from. Look for whole ingredients that are un-tampered with. And if you choose to eat something you know has unhealthy ingredients, then make sure you enjoy it, count it as a treat (or cheat meal), and make up for it moving forward at the next meal.

Protein

Protein is a nutrient that is essential to the body. Not only does it help in repair and build muscles, but thanks to protein our skin and bone health can be maintained. The immune system also requires protein to function optimally in warding off diseases. So, you may have questions about how to get protein, if you are new to a vegan diet. This is likely caused by the myth the body is not provided with sufficient nutrients in plant-based diets.

However, several plant foods will provide the protein needed in your diet, which include whole grains, vegetables, beans, nuts, peas, and soy products. When shopping and looking for proteins in vegetables, you should stock up on lentils, green peas, broccoli, cauliflower, yellow sweet corn, potatoes, Brussels sprouts, broccoli rabe, and avocado.

As you can see, when searching for protein in your diet, you have plenty of options to choose from. We can work out the math to figure out exactly how much protein you might need in your diet. The Dietary Reference Intakes suggest that the amount of protein you should consume everyday is equivalent to 0.8 grams per kilogram of your body weight, or 0.36 grams per pound. For example, if say you weigh 70 kilograms, you would multiply this by 0.8 grams to determine the daily protein quantity your body needs. In the case of 70 kilograms, the quantity of protein needed comes out to 72 grams.

The various foods mentioned above offer varying amounts of protein. This implies that combining several veggies will provide you with what you need. For instance, a one-cup serving of lentils provides you with 18 grams of the protein you need. On the other hand, a cup of green peas will only provide you with 8.5 grams of protein (Chertoff, 2016). Judging from the numbers, all you need is a mix of different plant foods to meet your daily protein intake.

Iron

Iron carries out various functions of in our bodies. This makes this nutrient necessary, as it is required for the production of blood and aids in the transportation of oxygen in the blood thanks to the production of hemoglobin. If there is not enough iron in the blood, the body will not obtain enough oxygen. Thanks to the presence of this nutrient in the body, the food we eat is also guaranteed to be easily converted into much needed energy. (Braun, L and Cohen, 2007; NHMRC (National Health and Medical Research Council 2005).

We should also remember that the body needs iron for cognitive functions. Some of those functions are learning, attention, alertness, problem-solving, and memory. Therefore, ensuring the ideal intake of iron means having optimal brain functioning.

The benefits mentioned above of iron go to show the importance of iron as a nutrient in our bodies. Unfortunately, the body doesn't naturally produce iron. Consequently, it is up to us to supplement it with good food choices. Plant foods that provide us with iron include legumes, vegetables, grains, and nuts and seeds.

Ideal legumes to shop for are lentils, tofu, lima beans, chickpeas, black beans, and soybeans. Here, the best grains to shop for include fortified cereals, oatmeal, brown rice, and quinoa. In terms of nuts and seeds, you should favor sunflower, pumpkin, pine, squash, cashews, and pistachios. In the vegetable category, on the other hand, Collard greens, Swiss chard, and tomato sauce are also excellent sources of iron.

Calcium

We usually think of milk when the word calcium comes up. That is because we have been taught that the best sources of calcium are dairy foods. That being true does not, however, mean that you cannot also obtain the nutrient from plant foods. By choosing certain plant foods, you have the added advantage of avoiding the negative health effects with which dairy and other animal products are associated.

Calcium is known to be crucial to our bone health and teeth development. It also plays an important role in regulating functions having to do with the heart, muscles, and nerves. The adult daily intake of calcium should be 1,000 mg, while children's daily intake should be even higher, about 1,300 mg (Jennings, 2018).

The best plant-based sources of calcium can be found in bok choy, broccoli, Chinese cabbage, beans, lentils, calcium-set tofu and fruits such as blackberries, blackcurrants, and raspberries.

Vitamin C

Vitamin C is vital for humans, and oranges, kiwis, broccoli, strawberries, and tomatoes are good plant sources of vitamin C.

Thankfully, Vitamin C is an easier nutrient to find in foods, as it is easily obtained in most fruits and vegetables. This vital vitamin helps maintain a strong immune system. Consequently, vitamin C is often used as a remedy for the common cold. Vegan foods we suggest you add to your diet are kiwi, Brussels sprouts, pineapple, broccoli, spinach, bell peppers, and oranges. From these foods you will obtain varying quantities of vitamin C. For example, a one-cup serving of broccoli give you about 80 mg of vitamin C. A higher quantity of Vitamin C can be obtained from a cup of kiwi as it provides you with nearly 170 mg of the nutrient (Von Alt, 2017).

Zinc

Zinc carries out vital functions in the body. As it cannot be produced naturally by your body, it is considered an essential nutrient that you must supplement in your diet. Zinc is the second most abundant mineral in the body after iron (Kubala, 2018). Zinc helps with immune functions, nerve function, metabolism, and digestion.

If you are wondering which foods are best to get zinc, they are whole grains, tempeh, lentils, tofu, seeds, nuts, peas, beans, as well as some fortified kinds of cereal. In some cases, zinc might not be easily absorbed by the body due to phytate compounds. Therefore, you should soak some of these foods, such as grains, seeds, and beans before cooking.

Chapter 4

WHAT TO EAT IN A WHOLE- FOOD, PLANT-BASED DIET

Those who love meat and fast food often struggle with starting a plant-based diet and sometimes even find it annoying. Doctors recommend reducing animal protein intake and maximizing plants, but how often have we ignored doctors' recommendations? In addition, it is not comfortable with the current fast-paced life, which gives no time to prepare a home-cooked meal.

Also, some people stay in places far away from farmers or where access to fresh farm produce is not easy; however, there are some tips you can use so that you do not run out of stock and start indulging. You can buy groceries in bulk worth one week and ensure you store them properly. Poor storage can spoil them, thus making them not suitable for human consumption.

Compared to fast and processed food, plant-based meals can be slightly expensive. That is why some people may be tempted to grab fast food during lunch, which is cheaper and readily available. It is thus useful to look at long-term benefits, potential risks, and your state of health. The cost of medication is or maybe even more expensive than plants and vegetables. This long-term benefit makes it worth investing in plant-based meals, which are fresh, nutritious, and healthy.

Kindly keep in mind that people with some of the diseases discussed above are not vegetarians, and this plant-based meal will not prevent one from getting those diseases, but the diet lowers the risk. Your doctor needs to give you consent if you're on medication or if you have some allergies, or just for the doctor to provide you with the approval that it's okay to start a plant-based meal.

Some people are allergic to grains or nuts; you can get a healthy alternative with better nutritional value. The plant should be included in the first meal of the day, breakfast. Include as much as you possibly can and make it delicious and appealing. If you don't know where to start, do not worry since the next chapters have some simple yet effective recipes that you can use. The recipes contain breakfast, lunch, and supper.

If you are doing a plant-based meal for health reasons, bring your family on board if possible; let them know why you have decided to change your eating habit. Chances are, they will be very appreciative and give you the necessary moral support. You'll also be helping them as they consume healthy plant meals, thus living healthier, fulfilling lives.

Family and friends can also recommend where to get fresh produce; they can motivate and encourage one another. Eating plant-based meals will help you realize a healthy lifestyle. Thus, people who live healthy lives have more fulfilling and rewarding lives; therefore, they are happier, content, and less anxious. They are also active and not conscious of their bodies since they are rarely overweight.

Not all plant-based meals are healthy in the same way, as not all animal protein is harmful. So, as you embark on a plant-based meal, confirm and recheck the quality and nutritional values. The best part about a plant-based diet is the low-calorie rate and is less fatty. Ensure that you take the recommended calories without overindulging or depriving yourself.

In a plant-based diet you are not permanently restricted from taking animal protein, but you can choose it in minimal quantities. It is good initially because it makes the meal plan workable and worth trying during the transition to a WFPB diet. This progressive process let you start slowly and do not necessarily cut on all at once animal protein intake.

Health workers are currently encouraging people who are not sick to eat healthy to boost their immunity and help their bodies fight some pathogens without medication. It is also interesting to note that medicines are made using herbs and some plants. So why wait to be sick if a plant-based meal can prevent some sickness?

Therefore, plant-based meals are an essential diet, and if everyone can get started, we can have a healthier nation. Moreover, it is one of the most inclusive vegetarian-related diets. Different places have different plants depending on the season, so you can take advantage of the season, purchase fresh and locally produced produce, and enjoy the raw nutrients.

Also, one can connect with local farmers and ensure that you get quality for your money, or instead of purchasing immediately, it's gotten from the farm and prepared the same day, thus preserving the nutrients. A plant-based meal is not easy but realistic and doable as long as you put your mind to it. So, redefine yourself today and start consuming a plant-based diet.

UNDERSTANDING YOUR FOOD

The Whole-Food Diet includes ingredients and recipes based on 4 principles that allow you to ensure the standard of the food you are eating.

Ideally, you should consume foods that satisfy the following 4 principles:

1. they promote a healthy psychological response from your body
2. they promote a healthy hormonal response
3. they improve the quality of your gut
4. they improve your immune function and minimize inflammation

The Whole Foods Diet is designed to target and improve specific aspects of our health. These aspects include:

- **Improving an unhealthy relationship with food:** Any psychological or emotional relationship you might have with unhealthy food could be greatly improved by eliminating nutrient-poor, calorie-dense food that promotes overconsumption in favor of the Whole-Food Diet.
- **Improving metabolism:** The meal plan and regulation that the Whole-Food Diet offers will lead to regular hormonal levels and regulate your blood sugar.
- **Improving the digestive system**
- **Soothing and calming an overactive Immune System:** The Whole-Food Diet is really an anti-Inflammatory diet that helps calm down an overactive immune system. As a consequence, symptoms, such as aches and pains, can be relieved through this diet.

YOUR WHY: MOTIVATION TO CHANGE

Adopting a new way of life can be many things. It can be intimidating and overwhelming. It can be scary or feel like the end of having fun eating. It can also be exciting at first and more difficult over time. Sometimes, adversity can make you question why you decided to make such a change in the first place.

Success in any area requires a significant amount of passion and motivation. You may set up everything else in your environment to aid your success, but it will be very difficult to stick with your plan when things get tough unless you have the right reason to want it so badly.

It is said that 80% of success is having a strong enough WHY (and the right mindset). Only 20% is reliant on mechanics or what you do. Having solid motivation will be something that you can come back to whenever you feel discouraged or frustrated.

You'll choose a motivation that comes from your heart and passion. Something with a whole lot of powerful emotion behind it: "I am a mother, so my daughter is a huge motivator". "I want to be my most healthy, so I can be there for her in every way".

Maybe you have a huge event or life change that you are preparing for. It can be a great opportunity to get healthier and into better shape. Some people have an ailment that has been tormenting them for some time. So, their reason behind going to a plant-based diet may be to experience living pain-free or without the symptoms or side effects.

Whatever the reason you want to do this, you should work toward building it up in your mind. First, gain massive leverage for yourself by making a list of everything you will gain by achieving your goals. Next, list what it will cost you not to make the change. What have you already lost or missed out on because you haven't changed?

You can even list the possible negativities you may experience by changing these aspects of your life. Then you can reexamine these negatives and see if they are worth keeping things the same over. If not, you can find a solution for them before they even become a problem.

Now that you have the proper drive (if you don't, go back and work on it until it is solid for you), set small, attainable goals. You will want to be able to track your progress and know that you are moving in the right direction that you want to go. If you aren't, you want to be able to catch it right away and correct it without too much delay.

You will want to keep a few things in mind with any goal and a few standard guidelines. First of all, you will want to focus on making SMART goals. It is a pretty common philosophy and helps achievement happen much quicker.

Your goals for adopting the plant-based lifestyle will be very personal and relative to you, depending on your lifestyle and what you want to achieve. Some people like to keep their current diet pretty much the same, only adopting a few foods or practices to enhance their health. Some like to change slowly and gradually until they've completely changed nearly every aspect of their previous diet. Still, others may already be well versed in plant-based living and wish to take their commitment even higher, adopting more healthy habits and dropping the disempowering ones.

Go at your own pace. Err on the scale's slower, more gradual side. Remember, slow and steady wins the race. What kind of race? The one you are running every single day of your life.

If you're still unsure of what specific goals you want to make, here are some examples:

Cut out and replace all dairy by September 17th this year (Maybe you'll know you've achieved your goal if you abstained from eating any dairy products for a whole month before your deadline, slowly tapering off until cutting it out completely.)

Lose X amount of excess weight or fat by May 6th this year. (You may know you've achieved this goal mainly by sticking to a wholesome, nutritious plant-based diet.)

Find X number of new fruits, vegetables, or plant-based products you love eating and incorporate them into a certain number of meals. (Or learn to cook or prepare it perfectly for a special event).

For each goal you have, go through each category and be sure you have a powerful reason for attaining it and keep it somewhere you can easily refer back to during this entire process.

HEALTHY FOODS

- **Vegetables:** You should always have the following on hand if you like them: spinach, broccoli, cauliflower, tomatoes, carrots, kale, peppers, and asparagus.
- **Whole Grains:** Stay away from the refined flours and eat only quinoa, pasta made with brown rice, farro, barley, brown rice, wild rice, rolled oats, buckwheat, amaranth, couscous, spelt, and Kamut.
- **Legumes:** Don't forget to have a lot of chickpeas, peas, black beans, peanuts, and lentils.
- **Fruits:** To get the vitamins and add some sweetness, eat bananas, citrus fruits, pears, apples, berries, and pineapples.
- **Starchy Vegetables**: These should not replace other vegetables but should be consumed. Eat squash, regular potatoes, and sweet potatoes.
- **Healthy Fats:** It is important to include healthy fats, such as unsweetened coconut, olive oils, avocados, and coconut oils.
- **Seeds:** Make sure you have a variety of nut butters and nuts that include almonds, Macadamia nuts, pumpkin seeds, sunflower seeds, almond butter, cashews, and tahini.
- **Plant-Based Milk:** You can drink any beverage that comes from nuts, such as cashew milk, coconut milk, and almond milk. Do not fall for the types that are sweetened in order to get used to the taste, as in the long-term, you will agree that the sweeteners used in these kinds of beverages are not good for your health. Hopefully soon, you could make your own homemade nut milk so that you can control how sweet it is.
- **Spices and Seasonings:** some great ones to always keep on hand are basil, rosemary, curry, sea salt, black pepper and turmeric (particularly great for reducing inflammation).
- **Drinks:** always opt for drinks that are unsweetened, like tea and coffee, freshly made fruit and vegetable juices or smoothies, plain water, and sparkling water. Some new brands of flavored and sparkling waters are sugar-free and help avoid drinking soda and sweetened juice. Always bear in mind that drinking a sufficient amount of water is important for your body's health. Besides, you can boost your immunity and help your body detox naturally just by adding ingredients, such as berries, sliced orange/lemon/ cucumber, mint, or lavender to your water as a combination altogether or individually to make it tasty.
- **Condiments:** A healthy diet does not mean a bland diet, so you can add condiments, such as vinegar (even apple cider vinegar), soy sauce (or tamari), vegan mayonnaise, mustard, salsa, lemon juice, and nutritional yeast.
- **Plant-based Proteins:** tofu and tempeh. This book provides great recipes for these protein-packed, plant-based options that are alternatives to meat.

UNHEALTHY FOODS

As a proponent of the WFPB diet, your primary focus should be on how to consume various plant-based meals in their most natural form. It means that you omit any contact or indulgence in heavily processed foods. And in case you are going to purchase your groceries, your main aim should be on fresh foods, and while buying foods that have been labeled, you should strictly aim for items that have the fewest possible ingredients.

- **Sweets and added sugars:** In this category anything that contains table sugar should be avoided, like cookies, cake, along with juice, sweet tea, candy, sugary cereals, etc.
- **Refined grains:** White pasta, white rice, bagels, and white bread.
- **Packaged foods:** Do not buy anything that resembles frozen dinners, cereal bars, crackers, chips etc.
- **Foods that are vegan-friendly but processed:** These will include vegan butter, faux cheeses, and plant-based imitation meats, capable of enticing you.
- **Artificial sweeteners**
- **Fast food:** Anything that comes from a fast food restaurant or certain foods you can buy from supermarkets like hot dogs, French fries, cheeseburgers, things like chicken nuggets, etc.
- **Processed animal products:** These include sausage, lunch meats, bacon, and beef jerky, among others.

TABLE OF FOODS

FOODS TO ELIMINATE	Seafood Beef Pork Mutton Game meats Poultry products Eggs Dairy products Refined Sugar Refined Grains	Protein Isolates: Pea protein isolate, Soy protein isolate, seitan. Beverages: Packaged fruit juice (even 100% pure fruit juice), Soda, sports drinks, energy drinks. High fructose corn syrup Partially hydrogenated oils Enriched/ bleached flours Foods enriched or fortified with unnatural vitamins Processed foods Salt
FOODS TO MINIMIZE	Refined white carbohydrates – like white rice, white bread, and white pasta. Sugary foods – swap them for fresh fruits, smoothies, freshly squeezed juices, etc. Avoid store-bought cakes, biscuits, pastries, soda, artificially flavored drinks, etc. Processed vegan and vegetarian alternatives that may include high amounts of salt and sugar. Greasy, fatty, and deep-fried foods – work with little amounts of fats as much as possible. Refined grains Honey Artificial sweeteners Frozen meals Crackers Breakfast bars	Snack foods Instant meals or microwaveable meals. White bread White flour White pasta White rice Glucose Sucrose Cane sugar Beet sugar Corn syrup Sorghum syrup Fruit juices with added sugar Table sugar Sugar cereals Candies Pastries Cakes Cookies

FOOD ALLOWED	Flax Seeds Almonds	Mandarin
	Pecans	Oranges Watermelon
	Brazil nuts Cashews Pistachios Walnut oil Sesame oil Avocado oil	Apples
	Chia seed oil	Berries Bananas Grapes
	Hemp seed oil Flaxseed oil	Melon
	Extra virgin olive oil (allowed in very small quantity during transition)	Avocados
		Lime
	Oats	Lemon Broccoli
	Quinoa Brown rice Spelt Buckwheat	Cauliflower
	Whole Grain bread Rye Barley	Kale Asparagus Carrots Tomatoes Peppers
	Almond milk Coconut milk	Butternut squash
	Soy milk	Zucchini Potatoes
	Rice milk	Beets
	Oat milk Hemp milk	Sweet potato Chickpeas Lentils
	Pine nuts	Peas
	Macadamia nuts	Black beans Kidney beans Chia Seeds Hemp Seeds
	Pumpkin Seeds	

PLANT-BASED SUPERFOODS

Dark Leafy Greens

Kale, Swiss chard, spinach, and collard greens are all classed as dark leafy greens, and these superfoods should be incorporated into your daily meal plan. They are a great digestive aid due to their high fiber content and dense sources of vitamins C and K, zinc, calcium, magnesium, iron, and folate. They also have a high antioxidant profile that assists the body in removing harmful free radicals.

Berries

Nature's little antioxidants are also the most delicious and delicate fruits we know. Berries host an array of benefits to the body, each with its special powers: Strawberries contain more vitamin C than oranges! They are antioxidant-rich and provide fiber, potassium, anthocyanins, and folate. Strawberries have excellent anti-inflammatory properties.

One of the foods that is richest in antioxidants is blueberries. They are also rich in vitamins C and K and manganese and support cognitive function and mental health.

Raspberries are rich in vitamin C, selenium, and phosphorus. Research shows they are beneficial in controlling blood sugar in people with diabetes. In addition, they are a great source of quercetin, which is known to slow the onset and growth of cancer cells. (Vafadar, A., Shabaninejad, Z., Movahedpour,2020)

Blackberries have high amounts of vitamins C and K and are incredibly high in great for receiving your dose of antioxidants and fiber as well as being loaded with phytochemicals.

Olive Oil

A staple of the Mediterranean diet for a reason, this oil is rich in antioxidants and monounsaturated fats that support cardiovascular health, prevent strokes and feed your hair and skin like nothing else. Despite being fat, it supports healthy weight maintenance. If you do not want to eliminate oil immediately, this can be one of your best choices. Only use it very rarely and in very small quantities, as well as coconut or avocado oil. I have put them (optional) in a few recipes to help you make this change a little less drastic.

Seaweed

It has been used in medicine for centuries, has antiviral properties, and has recently been tested positively in killing certain cancer cells. (El-Sheekh, M.M., Nassef, M., Bases 2022). Seaweed benefits cholesterol levels and is rich in antioxidants that are proven to lower heart disease. Seaweed is rich in vitamins A, C, D, E, K, and B. It's brimming with iron and iodine, essential for thyroid function, and has decent amounts of calcium, copper, potassium, and magnesium.

Avocado

Avocado is a great source of MUFAs (Monounsaturated Fatty Acids), which is vital for healthy cardiovascular function. Avocados facilitate vitamin and mineral absorption and also contain 20 vitamins and minerals. They lead to healthy hair, skin, and eyes, as well as fewer digestion issues. Anti-inflammatory properties and soluble fiber are also provided by this fruit.

Spirulina

Spirulina is a blue-green alga brimming with vitamins, minerals, and antioxidants. Algae are the greens of the sea and pack the same benefits as vegetables of the land in terms of being nutrient-dense, but something about growing under the sea makes them like the Superman of vegetables. They are a great supplemental form of protein and contain potassium, magnesium, calcium, iron, phosphorus, and vitamins A and C. They benefit the cardiovascular system by lowering the risk of cholesterol and high blood pressure. They also play a role in mental health by supporting serotonin production while working simultaneously to help eliminate heavy metals and toxins from the body.

SHOPPING LIST

Here are a few things that you should include in your shopping cart:

Any kind of fresh produce — both fruits and veggies. Go for dark, leafy greens. You should avoid eating avocados if you have a heart condition.

Go for dried lentils and beans. Were you to choose the canned version, it is best to shop for low-salt or low-sodium items. Rinse the beans well if they include salt.

Shop for raw nuts with no extra oil. Nut butter is also good but is high in calories, so use it cautiously. Instead, go for flax and chia seeds, sunflower, sesame, and pumpkin seeds.

Get dried fruits, but bear in mind that their calorie content is high, so they should be consumed cautiously.

Buy 100% whole-grain bread. Avoid wheat flour, enriched wheat flour, organic wheat flour, or unbleached wheat flour at all costs.

Look for whole grains that include quinoa, rice, farro, bulgur, hull-less barley, polenta, oatmeal, coarse cornmeal, and millet.

PLANNING PLANT-BASED MEALS

Meal planning lets you know which meals will be served on weekday evenings. It helps prepare a shopping list, minimize ready-to-eat meals, and put vegetables on the menu. Planning well also allows you to get ahead and prepare some dishes before you even start the week. But above all, it helps to clear the head of the famous question: "what are we eating tonight?"

Planning your plant-based meals leads to better eating, cutting down on delivered meals and, as a consequence, more money in your pocket. In addition, you will find you will feel less anxiety regarding cooking and what you are going to eat.

Why Plan Your Plant-Based Meals?

Planning your plant-based meals has many benefits. Here are some things you can do to enjoy delicious, well-prepared, plant-based meals. It helps you:

To avoid decision fatigue

When it's time for dinner, you've spent the day making decisions, big or small. Having to decide what you will eat at the last minute is additional stress that may lead you to draw pasta (or pizza delivery) for the umpteenth time!

By deciding in a quiet moment — on the weekend, for example — on your plant-based meals of the week, you will not have the evening only but also launch in the realization. It's simply liberating!

To limit food waste

Planning plant-based meals also take the time to take stock of what you already have in your refrigerator, freezer, and cupboard (or garden) and must be consumed more or less quickly. By the way, you will save money.

To eat more varied and balanced

By having visibility for several days on your meals, you will be able to identify the foods that come back often and that you could replace.

To get ahead

To have in mind or under the eyes the menus of the days to come also encourages to do small tasks ahead of time; cleaning a salad or plants and putting tofu to marinate. Little things in the evening will have saved you precious time.

How to Plan Your Meals?

I do not believe that there are infallible and universal Directions. The Right Direction is the one that suits you: you do not find it compelling, and it makes your life easier. The key is to get started without waiting to find the Directions. A sheet of paper and a pencil are enough!

Start by taking a calendar

Jot down anything that affects your schedule, such as professional and social commitments, school events, and so on. Consider the schedule of friends and family members if you share your meals with them. You can then make a note of them on the calendar and see on what days you'll have enough time to prepare a meal and when you'll have less time. This will allow you to plan your meals accordingly.

Choose recipes and go grocery shopping. Find plant-based meal ideas for each night, and list the ingredients you will need to purchase. Then, go grocery shopping with your list in hand to stock up. Having basic foods will make it easy for you, and you'll be able to prepare the week's dinners quickly. It will also save you time because there will be no need for daily grocery store runs. And because you'll know what to cook every night, you can open your fridge and start cooking once you're home.

Cook new recipes

Interest in books, magazines, and cooking shows continues to grow, and many parents have multiple home cooking books. But how often are these new recipes on the menu?

When planning the week's menu, this is the perfect time to flip through your books and put inspiring recipes on the menu. At the same time, you make the shopping list. Make sure to read the recipe. If it requires marinating the meat 12 hours in advance, it will be necessary to plan for it.

If you cook especially at the last minute, it is often the same recipes on the menu because they are the ones you know to do by heart. If they come back too often, you will feel bored because it seems like you're always eating the same thing. By including new recipes, the menu will be more varied, and it will also be more motivating to cook.

By planning meals well, it will also be possible to try to incorporate new dishes and foods on the menu — for example, vegetarian meals or a new vegetable.

Classic planning

You choose recipes, place them in your plan, and then draw up a shopping list. You can also use applications that offer integrated shopping lists and subscribe to meal planners who cook menus based on your preferences.

It can be a good idea for those who want to progress and repeatedly train on a type of dish. It allows you to search for ideas in a specific context. In short, you no longer go to the assault of bottomless pit recipes on the internet or even in your cookbooks without knowing where you go.

Meal planning is a key element in good food management. However, if you have tried several times to plan meals better, but the habit is still not anchored, there is surely something else that is not working.

Hence, the idea is to use a little of each approach while adapting to its concrete context: skills, constraints of the week, etc. Reviewing these different directions nevertheless seemed interesting to situate your practice, and I hope you open new horizons!

Chapter 5

TIPS AND STRATEGIES TO MANAGE FOOD CRAVINGS

t is not easy to make a change in any diet that you quickly embrace. The decision to take on a plant-based meal plan is based on wanting to live healthier lives. The change might be inevitable after many realizations of what we get when we eventually abandon what we prefer to consume. The previous chapters have narrowed down to health issues, with many studies leading to a better life by adopting the latter meal plan, which is plant-sourced.

Changing from regular life diets to start incorporating plant-based foods will meet some resistance at first if not well understood. Through this, we have come up with different tips to follow to start a plant-based diet. These several tips can help us make our understanding more comfortable when dealing with plant-based foods. These tips are also guidelines that will help us today and in the coming generations.

With that said, some people prefer a diet full of meat just because of its taste rather than understanding the health issues associated with its high consumption. These tips have been explained below in detail. The following chapters keenly highlight the need for easier comprehension so that each one of us can be better positioned to indulge in eating plant-based plant meals. After all, all of us need to begin from somewhere.

The first tip is about setting rules and ensuring that you are initiated to new plant-based meal recipes even twice a week. Regulations created by yourself will be quickly followed compared to the ones formed and forced on you. This plant-based diet is all about loving what you are doing. The created recipes will always be easy to follow, and once mastered, you will only be improving on them. One rule that can be created here is the setting of a day. This day is preserved mainly for one purpose: making a plant-based meal. Make it for the family and get their ultimate reviews on what you have made. Ask them to comment on the tastes and the food in general. The result will help you a lot, especially in your next meal.

The next tip is about creating a constant tendency towards plant-based meals. Make a plan for cooking this food more often within a week. Don't wait for ages to pass since you are induced to start your plant-based diet. Practice makes perfect, and your skills, especially necessary skills, will improve over time. Your experience will be a notch higher, reflected in your habits. Making cooking plant meals frequent is one of the best tips for jump-starting your plant-based meal. Along the way, you will get adapted to it. You'll also realize that you've changed your approach to how you always think of other types of food, such as diets full of meat and junk foods.

It's vital to grab recipes from the shelves or drawers where they are kept ready. The habit can occur without necessarily making or preparing these foods. At the same time, the pattern can improve your skills and give you several tips and morale to embark on preparation later on. Reading equips one with the skills and creativity needed in an area of expertise. You can now embark on that kitchen work after having enough knowledge and comprehension, especially on these plant-based recipes. Follow your recipes nice and slowly, and get used to them after some trials. The action will make it even easier. You will start enjoying it, and without knowing it, you will be in an excellent position to begin migrating from your current diet to plant-based diets.

Most of us use vegetables in our daily diets without knowing their value. We may also use the plants in meal preparation without having a real idea of what they do in our food. Some use vegetables because others have been using them, while others try to incorporate them just because they are there. It is good for your understanding of this, but if you want to jump-start this diet, then go for the vegetables that people consider unusual.

The ones that you have never used ever since you were born. The ones you have never even seen. Visit different fruit vendors' stores that have these unusual collections. Ask questions if you do not understand. Pick them and try using them to check on their flavors and tastes. Your ability to pick the right plant-based meal plan will help you choose which to use and which not to use. It is good to note that these unusual vegetables can be used to compensate for flavors obtained from meat-related dishes. This choice of particular types of plants is a good tip to start your plant-based diet.

As a beginner in this diet, the best tip for starting a plant-based diet meal plan will be, to begin with, vegetables. Try as much as possible to eat vegetables. The act can be during lunch and dinner or rather supper. Make sure that your plate is always full of plants of different categories. Different colors can help you choose the different types you want to learn. Vegetables can also be eaten as snacks, especially when combined with hummus or salsa. You can also use guacamole in this combination; rest assured, you will love it.

People eat meat on a daily basis. As said earlier, many prefer meat due to its taste. They don't go for it because of its nutritional value. In many cases, we can look for ways to change our thinking about meat. If we could all agree to reduce the level of intake of meat, our lives would be better. The reason is the health benefits of eating vegetables, not meat.

The action might cause some depression and stress. It's good to note that you are not supposed to withdraw all meat at once. In this case, you can change your approach toward meal intake. Reducing consumption levels will help us indulge in a plant-based cooking meal plan. You can also use this meat as just a side dish. That's like garnish. Avoid using meat as a centerpiece.

The types of fats and oils being used should be highly considered. Well-chosen fats or oils will come from avocados, olive oil, specific seeds, and even nuts like groundnuts. By doing this, you will be in a high position of being initiated to plant-based cooking.

As we all know, changing from one diet to another will be challenging. The case is specific, especially within a short period. You need to cook at least twice, thrice, or even once within a week. Cook some plant-based food once or twice a week, depending on how you want it.

You will learn how to jump-start your initiation period. You'll also understand what it takes to grasp the basic knowledge of plant-based meal planning.

Try to use more vegetables, beans, and even whole grains in most cases. Never use processed foodstuffs like processed and refined flour since this has got fewer nutrients and mostly lacks enough fiber needed within the body.

Another tip that will help you start a plant-based diet meal is using whole grains during breakfast. Use it in high quantities since it will help you adopt this kind of diet within a short period. It is not always easy to use all of these whole grains. The best way forward is to choose meals that can suit you and the rest of your family at first. Good examples will be highly recommended. These might include oats, barley, or even buckwheat. Here, you can add flavors provided by different nuts and several seeds. Don't forget to include fresh fruits next to your reach.

Greens are some of the best vegetables preferable in the plant-based diet. They are also crucial in helping you to maintain a healthy diet. And going for them will help you jump-start your long journey in embracing plant-based foods. Greens can be used at different levels, and embracing them at the initial level is the best. So go for greens such as kale, spinach, collards, and much more.

Use a good cooking mode to preserve their nutritional value, tastes, and flavors. Excellent cooking methods for food can include using steam, grilling, or even frying for a short period. All the mentioned cooking or preparation styles will help maintain the nutrients in these greens. The body tissues readily require these nutrients for the body organs to function the way they should.

Another way to get induced to a plant-based diet is by using diets that revolve around or contain salad. You can make the salad greens from leafy greens like spinach romaine, and sometimes the red leafy greens are preferred. Different kinds of vegetables are added here. These vegetables are added together with beans, peas, or fresh herbs.

The best thing about fruits is that fruits are practical, allowing you to consume them at any time and in any way. They don't have any form of rigid procedure or protocol that needs to be followed as far as their consumption is concerned. Eating fruits daily as dessert will help you adapt to them. It will create some habits within you, and without realizing it, you will be fully indulged in a plant-based meal.

Fruits play different roles in our diet plans. By consuming them every day, we can quickly boost our immunity. The same meals will help us forget to focus more on eating healthy for the rest of our lives. For example, some fruits will help you reduce your craving for sugary sweets, especially after having the main meal. Fruits such as watermelon and apples can help in keeping hydrated. Therefore, you will be able to get used to it. In the long run, you will be adapted to plant-based diet meals.

Another way to help you start your meal plan is having curiosity instead of being extra curious. Many studies have proof of interest as a tip in starting plant-based meal plans. Sometimes in life, you want to venture into something you never knew. You want to do something that you have not been doing, especially when cooking different meal plans.

Sometimes you can jump-start this plant meal as a result of love. Many people are trying something new. If you love plant-related dishes, you will be in an excellent position to embrace them after some time. The move will help you manage your eating habits.

Embracing plant-based diet meal plans will come in handy with the food sector's broader choice. You will have an alternative food source in addition to what you have been consuming over the last few years. Being led by your love to eat plant-based meals or change your diet will vastly help you get used to it.

In the long run, you will get familiarized and used to it. You will then start practicing it in your daily routines, thus reducing your urge for meat-related meals. Of course, for this one to work better, you must love eating too. The eventual result is just an aspect of life that will accelerate your objective of starting plant-based diet meal plans.

Another tip is about pairing foods. You can use this tool to know better which plant-based foods can be matched and which result in good taste. You can do this pairing by combining several flavors. The result should give you a strong feeling that works for you.

Trial and error work. When you comprehend food pairing completely, rest assured that your cooking skills and love of it are moving to the next level. The latter will enable you to cook your plant-based meal without checking or following your recipes. You shall also experience timely results in time reduction and save energy too. Sometimes, you also need to compare notes on different books about plant-based recipes and pick only the best that can help you begin on this.

You can choose a paper with a Mediterranean diet and another with vegetarian food recipes or go for the Nordic diet. Compare the notes and pick the similarities. The actions will make you understand much more about plant-based food and how to prepare them adequately. These books by different authors will also help you with inspiration and ideas on different flavors.

Watching shows is another tip that will help you start plant-based meal plans. Have those videos concerning cooking at your reach. Several stations deal with cooking. Spend much time watching them as you take notes. Make a date with your television and watch those food networks that talk much about plant-based diets.

Many studies have concluded that cooking videos are essential, especially in learning cooking. It is because, in your mind, you will be in a position to know what the food will look like even if you are not cooking. Using videos creates some perfection in the kitchen. You'll have no stress or pressure here. It is all about watching and doing the required practice. Practicing now and then gives you that experience you need and will later help you embrace the plant-based diet.

TIPS AND STRATEGIES FOR GETTING STARTED

Find Your Motivation

Before making any dietary changes, it is essential to take a step back and determine why you need to take this step. What is your motivation behind trying a plant-based diet? Maybe you are suffering from a disease, which is the best strategy for you to reduce the effects of the disease. Perhaps, instead, you are looking for a way to improve your health to your overall wellbeing. Being healthy means having a good heart.

Start Slow

It is the second most important consideration you should bear in mind. You need to initiate your transition slowly. Select a few plant-based foods and begin rotating them for about a week. A good tip here is to select foods that you often enjoy. They can range from lentil stew, oatmeal, jacket potatoes, beans, or veggie stir-fry. Human beings are creatures of habit.

Cut Down on Meat and Processed Foods

A slow transition guarantees that your body adapts well to the change in diet. In line with this, you shouldn't just avoid processed foods and meat from the get-go. Proceed gradually. Begin by cutting down on your meat intake. Next, increase the portions of veggies on your plate while reducing the meat portions. After some time, get rid of them entirely, as you will have gained the perception that you can do without them. Later on, work on your recipes. For example, if you were a huge fan of beef chili, you could swap the meat with portobello mushrooms. The idea is to continue eating your favorite meals as a plant-based version of what you used to have.

Surround Yourself with Wholesome Foods

If you are going to adopt a healthy lifestyle, you must surround yourself with healthy foods. In this case, no other forms of food will be okay; you should only have plant-based foods. Walk around your kitchen as you try and evaluate whether the foods around you are helpful to your goal. If not, don't hesitate to throw them away or donate them. Just because you bought them doesn't imply that you will be wasting food if you choose not to eat them.

Watch Your Protein Portions

The Dietary Reference Intake recommends that the average amount of protein the body needs is about 0.8 grams per kilogram. That implies that the typical, sedentary man will require about 56 grams daily protein intake, whereas a woman will require about 46 grams (Gunnars, 2018). That shows that we only need a fraction of our protein intake to supplement the body with what it needs. Unfortunately, most dieters overconsume proteins with the idea that the body requires nutrients. We forget that too much of something can be toxic and dangerous.

Whether the body needs it or not, watching our portions is vital. While striving to live on a plant-based diet, you should be careful of the amounts of protein you consume. Excessive intake will undeniably lead to negative health effects. You must ensure that your plant foods have enough calories to provide your body with energy for metabolism and other purposes.

Educate Yourself

In addition to focusing on food, you should also invest your time and money in educating yourself, just like you are doing by reading this book. Unfortunately, digital media and advertising has polluted our minds. Industrial food producers want to keep us far from realizing that plant-based foods are the best for our bodies and the planet we live on.

Find Like-Minded People

Relating to like-minded individuals will be helpful in good and bad times. These are people who are also looking to reap the benefits of eating a plant-based diet. Therefore, by relating to them, you can share success stories and help each other in times of need. With the advent of the Internet, it should not be difficult for you to find other people who are vegetarians. Browse through social media pages and join their groups. Here, you will find significant information about your new diet plan. For instance, some people will be eager to share tasty, plant-based recipes with you.

Get your Fiber

Fiber is a key component in any diet. It helps to regulate your digestive system, eliminate toxins from your body, maintain a healthy weight and even prevent disease.

Hydration is Important

Your muscles thrive on hydration and need plenty of cool water before stepping foot in the gym. Consistently refuel your body with water. At least every 20 minutes during the workout and continue for as long as possible after your workout. Your body will let you know when you have not had enough hydration. A few of the signs of dehydration include:

- Cramps
- Dizziness or loss of balance
- Incredible fatigue

If you dislike the taste of plain water or get bored, you can add a few squeezes of fresh lemon to your water to give it a little taste and the added benefits of extra vitamins while you work out.

Purge Your Kitchen

You should eliminate any temptation in your kitchen and call your name if you're trying to start a plant-based diet. It's not good to have unhealthy foods in front of you, or you're bound to give in.

Plan Your Meals

Luckily, this book comes with a meal plan to help you stick to your first 3 weeks of diet. However, you may want to stick to planning your meals for the first few months if you find yourself struggling.

Clean the Pantry

I want you to look at this day as day number one from now on! There is no looking back and no turning around from this point. The best tip I can provide is to clean out your pantry and fridge as soon as possible. Whether you recycle, toss, or donate, just eliminate the non-compliant items! You will want to eliminate anything from white bread, deli meats, dairy products, processed foods, and sugary drinks. You will make room for the good when you get rid of the bad.

Create your meal plan

In this case, you will be following mine at first. As you plan your meals, this will help you restock your fridge and pantry now that you have removed all the unhealthy items.

As you practice the plant-based diet for longer, you will learn some of your favorite staples to keep in stock. Remember that there is no reason to make your diet too complicated. Some popular staples will include fresh fruits, oats, beans, and seeds.

Spend Time Finding Recipes

When you are first starting a plant-based diet, it will be important that you go in with a plan! The best way to do this will be to spend some time on the Internet (or this book), finding some plant-based recipes that you want to try.

Slow Down When Shopping

As you begin the plant-based diet, you may be surprised to learn about some foods you never thought about purchasing before. So often, when we get to the grocery store, we want to be in and out so that we can get home, but now, I suggest you slow down and spend some extra time in the grocery store.

Now that you are eating more whole foods, selecting products that will benefit you will be important. As you stroll through the produce section, spend even an extra 12 minutes checking out ingredients such as tempeh, quinoa, and different plant-based milk for you to try. As you expand your horizons, you never know what will become a new favorite in your diet!

Simple Salads

When you are first starting a plant-based diet, it is all too easy to become overly eager to get to planning intense meals for the week. If you feel this way, I want to ensure you understand that it is perfectly okay to keep your meals simple! For this reason, I highly suggest you incorporate eating a salad daily.

As you plan grocery shopping for the week, choose some salad bar choices to keep the salads fresh and exciting. Salads are easy to whip together and can be transported on the go when you need a healthy lunch at work or on the road.

FOOD-BASED MISTAKES TO AVOID

Pursuing a plant-based diet plan is a complete lifestyle, not just a temporary habit. If you treat it temporarily, you get the results for a shorter time and end up returning from where you started. You might find it a bit hard initially, but hard work always pays off. The following commonly committed mistakes are known to be a major demotivation for getting you off the plan. Avoid these mistakes at the most to make your life healthy and organic. These include:

Not Having a Support Group

You are going to need immense support. Starting a new thing without any support and not having like-minded individuals around you can be very problematic. Find someone who shares the same thoughts, or identical approaches, so that they can keep you motivated.

You can opt for various classes based on plant-based diet plan foods in your locality, join various online groups, have a follow-up on various social media influencers who have adopted the same diet plan, and much more.

Not Adjusting to the Shift

You start gradually with your diet plan. Any abrupt or massive change in your already adapted diet plan will intrigue your reptilian brain to oppose it in the first place. Having a gradual approach can let you follow the plan more profoundly and systematically healthy.

Prepping the Same Food, But with Plants

You can try out plant-based alternatives of pizzas and burgers and blend in with new tastes. But it is crucial to understand that a plant-based alternative isn't going to taste exactly like bacon, cheese-dominated pizza, and much more. The good thing is that plants offer many new flavors, which are delicious, of course.

You can add various herbs to make your food taste more delicious. For example, you can opt for oregano with Italian cuisines, go for cumin and turmeric with Indian cuisines, etc., the only mantra is to be patient, and soon you are going to enjoy your diet plan.

You can also experience a little hunger because your body is digesting and detoxifying. Hunger is just a phase, and it will come and move away.

Not Being Prepared for the Plan

Not being prepared to adapt to the plan is the main reason for failure in following the plan in the first place. Food planning is very easy and can prove beneficial when following a plant-based diet plan. You can add healthy foods like veggies, seeds, nuts, lentils, beans, fruits, and berries to your food list and enjoy a superb meal plan based on purely plant-based ingredients.

You can go for various plant-based recipes on various online forums, ask your friends who have followed the diet, and any other relevant place you can find so. The agenda is to plan your meals, make grocery lists, and start prepping them.

You can keep your plan very simple and easy at the start to avoid any incontinence and later keep on adding various other recipes to make your plan more colorful.

Recruiting Others

It is also a very common mistake committed by people. You can only shift to the plant-based diet plan with your own will, and only that will make it successful for you. Trying to recruit others might initiate a process of resistance and resentment, which can lead your plan to fail. If you need support, try searching for it in those individuals who share a similar mindset as yours.

Eating Processed Foods

A plant-based diet plan means having a healthier mind and body. However, people complain about it being less convenient because they are inclined to eat pre-packaged foods. Instead, you should go for fresh veggies, fruits, seed butter, and nuts. Also, you can make so many simpler fresh dips, just like hummus. You can also keep various jars to keep your food in them and take them with you when you are on the move.

Chapter 6
WHOLE FOOD PLANT-BASED DIET RECIPES

This book and the recipes in it are SOS-free oriented. However, it is understandable that going from a diet rich in animal food and even junk food to such drastic deprivation in a short time can be unsustainable for some people.

So, to help in the transition process, some recipes have a few tablespoons of oil among the ingredients, which can still be optional for those who want to eliminate it.

Similarly, salt and sugar have been eliminated. Even for these ingredients, if you do not feel ready and prefer to eliminate them little by little gradually, you can consider adding them extra, in modest amounts, to the recipes and then gradually eliminate them. Of course, the ideal solution would be not to do so. The goal is to achieve the result of arriving at an SOS-free plant-based diet. How much time can it take? The freedom is left to each person to follow his or her own pace. It is certainly better to take a few months and follow a gradual path than to follow the diet narrowly for 15 to 20 days and then quit forever.

Changing bad habits acquired over many years in a short time is not easy, but with one step at a time, you will surely achieve the goal of healthy living and eating. Use these recipes as a simple first guide. Then, feel free to change the ingredients, replace, for example, broccoli with zucchini for soup or pasta, one type of fruit with another for ice cream, and the recipes will still work.

Use as much food as possible in your local area and follow seasonal availability for the freshest, most natural food possible. With simplicity, you will be able to vary your menu. Enjoy the path to a healthier and happier life!

BREAKFAST

Pineapple and Mango Oatmeal

Preparation: 5 Minutes	Cooking: 0 Minutes	Servings: 2

INGREDIENTS

- 2 cups unsweetened almond milk
- 2 cups rolled oats
- ½ cup pineapple chunks, thawed if frozen
- ½ cup diced mango, thawed if frozen
- 1 banana, sliced
- 1 tbsp chia seeds
- 1 tbsp agave syrup

DIRECTIONS

1. Stitir together the almond milk, oats, pineapple, man
go, banana, chia seeds and agave syrup in a large bowl or Mason jar untitil you see no clumps.
2. Cover and refrigerate to chill for at least 4/5 hours or more
3. Serve chilled with your favorite toppings.

Nutritional Facts: Calories 512; Fat 22.1 g; Carbohydrates 13.1 g; Protein 14.1 g

Southwestern Tofu Scramble

Preparation: 15 minutes	Cooking: 10 minutes	Servings: 4

INGREDIENTS

- 14 oz. extra-firm tofu
- ¼ cup vegetable broth (use low-sodium vegetable broth during transition if necessary, avoid salt)
- 1 red onion, diced
- 1 red bell pepper, thinly sliced
- ½ cup cremini mushrooms, chopped
- ¼ cup nutritional yeast
- 1 tsp garlic powder
- 1 tsp cumin powder
- ½ tsp smoked paprika
- ½ tsp chili powder
- ½ tsp crushed red pepper
- ¼ tsp turmeric
- Black pepper, to taste
- Optional toppings: salsa, cilantro, hot sauce

DIRECTIONS

1. Pat the tofu dry and absorb any excess liquid with a paper towel or clean cloth. Set aside. Heat a large skillet over medium heat.
2. Sauté the onions, red bell pepper and mushrooms in the vegetable broth for approximately 5 minutes.
3. Take the tofu and crumble it into bite-sized pieces into the skillet. Add the nutritional yeast and seasonings and cook for another 5 to 7 minutes until the tofu is slightly browned.
4. Top with salsa, cilantro, or hot sauce. Serve immediately with breakfast potatoes, toast, or fruit.

Nutritional Facts: Calories 116; Fat 2 g; Carbohydrate 11 g; Protein 14 g

Indian-Inspired Tofu Scramble

Preparation: 10 minutes	Cooking: 15 minutes	Servings: 4

INGREDIENTS

- 2 tbsp vegetable broth or water
- 1 cup diced yellow onion
- ¾ cup diced carrot
- ½ cup diced celery
- 1 (13,5-oz.) block extra-firm tofu, pressed and drained
- 1 tsp ground turmeric
- ½ tsp smoked paprika
- ½ tsp chili powder
- 1 ½ cups chopped kale
- ½ tsp Spicy Umami Blend

DIRECTIONS

1. Heat up your broth on medium-high heat in a large skillet. Add the chopped onion, carrot and celery, and sauté for about 3 minutes until the onion begins to soften.
2. With your hands, crumble the tofu into the skillet. Add the spices while stirring well. Cook for 5 minutes.
3. Add the kale and stir. Cover the skillet, put the heat on medium-low, and cook for an additional 5 minutes. Stir in the seasoning and serve warm.

Nutritional Facts: Calories 125; Fat 7 g; Protein 11 g; Carbs 9 g

Indian-Style Lentil and Potato Hash

Preparation: 10 minutes	Cooking: 15 minutes	Servings: 4

INGREDIENTS

- ¼ cup vegetable broth/water, plus more if needed
- 1 (10-oz.) russet potato, unpeeled, cut into ¼-inch pieces
- 1 tsp ground cumin
- ½ tsp ground allspice
- ½ tsp ground ginger
- ½ tsp garam masala
- ½ tsp Spicy Umami Blend (optional)
- 1 (15-oz.) can brown lentils, drained and rinsed
- ½ cup chopped green onions
- ½ cup chopped fresh cilantro (optional)

DIRECTIONS

1. Warm the broth over medium-high heat in a large skillet. Add the potato, cumin, allspice, ginger and garam masala, and cook, frequently stirring, until the potato is tender for about 10 minutes. Put more broth or water as needed to maintain a very thick sauce consistency.
2. Add the lentils and stir to combine. Adjust the heat to medium, cover, and then cook for 5 minutes more.
3. Divide the lentil mixture among four bowls. Top each serving with 2 tbsp of green onions and 2 tbsp of cilantro, then serve.

Nutritional Facts: Calories 148; Fat 1 g; Protein 8 g; Carbs 29 g

Morning Muesli

Preparation: 30 minutes   **Cooking: 20 minutes**   **Servings: 5**

INGREDIENTS

- ½ cup dry millet
- 2 cups rolled oats
- 1 cup chopped walnuts
- ½ cup pure agave syrup
- 1 cup chopped pitted dates

DIRECTIONS

1. Preheat the oven to 350°F. Prepare your baking sheet lined using parchment paper or a silicone baking mat. Rinse the millet, drain, and shake off as much water as possible. Heat a medium skillet over medium-high heat.
2. Put the millet in the hot skillet and cook, frequently stitirring, untitil it becomes dry and aromatitic and begins
   to make popping noises, 5 to 8 minutes. Immediately transfer the millet to a large bowl and let cool for 10 minutes.
3. Add the oats, walnuts and agave syrup, and stitir untitilwell combined. Transfer the muesli to the prepared
   baking sheet and bake for 18 minutes.
4. Place the baking sheet on a wire rack and let it cool. Stitir in the dates, then transfer the muesli to an air
   titight container.

Nutrititional Facts: Calories 515; Fat 18 g; Protein 12 g; Carbs 82

Fruity Yogurt Parfait

Preparation: 5 minutes   **Cooking: 0 minutes**   **Servings: 2**

INGREDIENTS

- 2 cups plain plant-based yogurt or Cashew Cream
- 2 cups fresh blueberries or raspberries
- 1 cup agave muesli or granola
- ¼ tsp ground cinnamon

DIRECTIONS

1. In an individual serving bowl or parfait glass, layer

½ cup of yogurt, 1 cup of berries, ½ cup of muesli, another ½ cup of yogurt, and 1/8 tsp of cinnamon. Repeat in a second serving bowl or parfait glass.

Nutritional Facts: Calories 520; Fat 30 g; Protein 14 g; Carbs 71 g

Apple Avocado Toast

Preparation: 5 minutes   **Cooking: 2 minutes**   **Servings: 4**

INGREDIENTS

- 1 large ripe avocado, halved and pitted
- 1 small apple, cored
- 2 tbsp lemon juice
- ½ cup chopped pecans
- ½ tsp ground cinnamon
- 4 slices whole-grain bread, toasted

DIRECTIONS

1. Scoop your avocado flesh into a small bowl, then mash it with a fork. Cut the apple into 1/8-inch cubes and add it to the avocado.
2. Add the lemon juice, pecans and cinnamon, and gently fold with a rubber spatula until well combined.
3. Spread about ¼ cup of the apple-avocado mixture onto each slice of toast and serve.

Nutritional Facts: Calories 276; Fat 19 g; Protein 7 g; Carbs 25 g

Banana-Nut Butter Boats

Preparation: 5 minutes   **Cooking: 5 minutes**   **Servings: 2**

INGREDIENTS

- 4 large bananas, peeled
- ½ cup natural or homemade peanut butter
- 1 tbsp unsweetened cocoa powder
- 1 to 2 tbsp unsweetened soy milk
- ¼ tsp ground cinnamon

DIRECTIONS

1. Slice your bananas in half lengthwise. Process the peanut butter, cocoa powder and 1 tbsp of soy milk in a food processor or blender until thick but easy to pour.
2. Add more soy milk, if needed, to get the right consistency. Set aside. Heat a large skillet over medium-high heat.
3. When a few drops of water quickly bubble up on the surface, place the banana halves cut-side down in the skillet and cook for 1 minute, then turn and cook for 1 minute more.
4. Place 4 banana halves on each of the two plates, cut-side up. Drizzle about half the sauce over each plate. Sprinkle a pinch or two of ground cinnamon over each plate and serve.

Nutritional Facts: Calories: 635; Fat 34 g; Protein 18 g; Carbs 78 g

Oatmeal-Raisin Breakfast Bowl

Preparation: 5 minutes   **Cooking: 30 minutes**   **Servings: 4**

INGREDIENTS

- 1 cup steel-cut oats
- 2 cups unsweetened non-dairy milk
- ½ cup raisins
- 1 tsp ground cinnamon
- ¼ cup chopped pitted dates
- ¼ cup chopped pecans

DIRECTIONS

1. Mix the oats, milk, raisins and cinnamon in a large saucepan, and boil over medium-high heat.
2. Adjust the heat to low, then simmer, occasionally stirring, until the oats are tender, about 25 minutes. Remove from the heat. Stir in the dates and pecans, and serve.

Nutritional Facts: Calories 355; Fat 9 g; Protein 10 g; Carbs 61 g

Hot and Spicy Savory Oats

Preparation: 15 minutes   **Cooking: 30 minutes**   **Servings: 4**

INGREDIENTS

- 1 small yellow onion, diced
- 1 large red bell pepper, seeded and diced
- 1 large jalapeño, seeded and minced, divided
- 2 cups vegetable broth
- 1 cup steel-cut oats
- 1 cup fresh baby spinach
- 1 ½ tbsp nutritional yeast
- 1 tsp Spicy Umami Blend
- 1 large tomato, chopped
- 1 tsp lime juice

DIRECTIONS

1. In a large saucepan, sauté the onion, half of the jalapeño, and the bell pepper over medium-high heat for about 5 minutes. Add the broth and oats and bring to a boil.
2. Bring the heat down and simmer, stirring occasionally, until the oats are tender, about 25 minutes. Remove from the heat. Stir in the spinach and nutritional yeast, cover, and let sit for 5 minutes.
3. Mix the tomato, the remaining half of jalapeño and lime juice in a small bowl. Serve the oats with salsa on top.

Nutritional Facts: Calories 202; Fat 2 g; Protein 8 g; Carbs 39 g

Macro Miso Breakfast Soup

Preparation: 15 minutes   **Cooking: 10 minutes**   **Servings: 4**

INGREDIENTS

- 1 (3-inch) piece kombu
- 1 large carrot, unpeeled, chopped (about ½ cup)
- 1 large celery stalk, chopped (about ½ cup)
- 1 small sweet potato, unpeeled, cut into ½-inch cubes (about 1 cup)
- 2 tsp ground ginger
- 8 oz. baby bok choy, halved lengthwise and coarsely chopped
- ¼ cup red miso paste
- 1 tbsp rice vinegar

DIRECTIONS

1. In a large saucepan, combine the Kombu and 4 cups of water, and bring to a boil over medium-high heat. Adjust the heat to medium, cover, and cook for 1 minute. Remove the kombu, set it aside, and pour the broth into a large measuring cup.
2. Pour about ¼ cup of broth back into the saucepan and heat over medium-high heat. Add the carrot, celery, sweet potato and ginger, and cook, frequently stirring, until the sweet potato is fork-tender, about 5 minutes.
3. Pour the rest of the broth into your saucepan and bring to a boil. Add the bok choy, lower the heat to medium, and cook until wilted, about 3 minutes.
4. Remove the saucepan from the heat. Spoon about 1 cup of broth into a bowl or measuring cup. Add the miso to the cup of broth and whisk until dissolved.
5. Pour the miso broth back into the pan, add the vinegar, and stir to combine. Ladle into bowls and serve.

Nutritional Facts: Calories 103; Fat 1 g; Protein 4 g; Carbs 18 g

Golden Porridge

Preparation: 5 minutes   **Cooking: 60 minutes**   **Servings: 4**

INGREDIENTS

- ½ cup dry short-grain brown rice, rinsed and drained
- ½ cup dry farro, rinsed and drained
- 1 tsp ground turmeric
- ½ cup fresh or thawed frozen corn
- 4 cups loosely packed shredded collard greens
- ¼ cup unsweetened non-dairy milk
- 1 to 2 tsp low-sodium soy sauce or tamari (optional)
- 2 tsp sesame seeds

DIRECTIONS

1. In a large saucepan, add rice, farro, and 2 cups water and bring to a boil over medium-high.
2. Lower the heat to low, cover, and simmer until the rice is tender and the farro is just chewy for 45 to 50 minutes. Remove from the heat.
3. Add the turmeric, corn and collard greens to the grains, and stir gently with a fork to combine. Cover and let sit for 15 minutes.
4. Return the saucepan to medium-low heat. Add the milk and soy sauce (if using) and cook, frequently stirring, until thick and creamy, about 5 minutes. Spoon the porridge into bowls, garnish with the sesame seeds, and serve.

Nutritional Facts: Calories 197; Fat 2 g; Protein 7 g; Carbs 40 g

SOUPS, STEWS, CHILIES

Vegetable Broth Sans Sodium

Preparation: 5 minutes   **Cooking: 60 minutes**   **Servings: 1 cup**

INGREDIENTS

- 5 sprigs dill
- 2 freshly sliced yellow onions
- 4 chives
- 6 freshly peeled and sliced carrots
- 10 cups water
- 4 freshly sliced celery stalks
- 3 cloves freshly minced garlic
- 4 sprigs parsley

DIRECTIONS

1. Put a large pot on medium heat and stir the onions. Fry the onions for 1 minute until they become fragrant. Add the garlic, celery, carrots and dill along with the chives and parsley, and cook everything. You will know that the mix is ready when it becomes fragrant.
2. Add the water and allow the mixture to boil. Reduce the heat and allow everything to cook for 45 minutes.
3. Turn off the heat. The broth will cool in about 15 minutes.
4. Strain the broth with the help of a sieve so that you have a clear vegetable broth.
5. If you are not using the broth right away, store it as ice cubes. You can store the ice cubes for a week.

Nutritional Facts: Calories 362; Carbs 21 g; Protein 12 g; Fat 21 g

Broccoli Fennel Soup

Preparation: 15 Minutes   **Cooking: 10 Minutes**   **Servings: 4**

INGREDIENTS

- 1 fennel bulb, white and green parts coarsely chopped
- 10 oz. broccoli, cut into florets
- 3 cups vegetable stock
- Freshly ground black pepper
- 1 garlic clove
- 1 cup dairy-free cream cheese
- 3 oz. vegan butter
- ½ cup chopped fresh oregano

DIRECTIONS

1. Combine the fennel, broccoli, vegetable stock and black pepper in a medium pot. Bring to a boil until the vegetables soften; 10 to 15 minutes.
2. Stir in the remaining ingredients and simmer the soup for 3 to 5 minutes.
3. Adjust the taste with black pepper, and dish the soup.
4. Serve warm.

Nutritional Facts: Calories 240; Fat 0 g; Protein 0 g; Carbs 20 g

Coconut and Grilled Vegetable Soup

Preparation: 10 Minutes **Cooking: 45 Minutes** **Servings: 4**

INGREDIENTS

- 2 small red onions cut into wedges
- 2 garlic cloves
- 10 oz. butternut squash, peeled and chopped
- 10 oz. pumpkins, peeled and chopped
- 4 tbsp melted vegan butter
- Black pepper, to taste
- 1 cup water
- 1 cup unsweetened coconut milk
- 1 lime juiced
- ¾ cup vegan mayonnaise (preferably home made)
- Toasted pumpkin seeds for garnishing

DIRECTIONS

1. Preheat the oven to 400°F.
2. On a baking sheet, spread the onions, garlic, butternut squash and pumpkins, and drizzle half of the butter on top. Season with black pepper and rub the seasoning well onto the vegetables. Roast in the oven for 45 minutes or until the vegetables are golden brown and softened.
3. Transfer the vegetables to a pot; add the remaining ingredients except for the pumpkin seeds. Then use an immersion blender to puree the ingredients until smooth.
4. Dish the soup, garnish with the pumpkin seeds and serve warm.

Nutritional Facts: Calories 290; Fat 10 g; Protein 30 g; Carbs 0 g

Mixed Berries Stew

Preparation: 10 minutes **Cooking: 15 minutes** **Servings: 6**

INGREDIENTS

- 1 lemon zest, grated
- Juice 1 lemon
- ½ pint blueberries
- 1 pint strawberries halved
- 2 cups water
- 2 tbsp coconut sugar

DIRECTIONS

1.
   the other ingredients.
2. Bring to a simmer and cook over medium heat for 15 minutes.
3. Divide into bowls and serve cold.

Nutritional Facts: Calories 172; Fat 7 g; Fiber 3.4 g; Carbs 8 g; Protein 2.3 g

Tofu Goulash Soup

Preparation: 35 Minutes   **Cooking: 20 Minutes**   **Servings: 4**

INGREDIENTS

- 2 cups tofu
- 4 ¼ oz. vegan butter
- 1 white onion, chopped
- 2 garlic cloves, minced
- 1 ½ cup butternut squash
- 1 red bell pepper, deseeded and chopped
- 1 tbsp paprika powder
- ¼ tsp red chili flakes
- 1 tbsp dried basil
- ½ tbsp crushed cardamom seeds
- Black pepper, to taste
- 1 ½ cup crushed tomatoes
- 3 cups vegetable broth
- 1½ tsp red wine vinegar
- Chopped parsley, to serve

DIRECTIONS

1. Place the tofu between two paper towels and allow water to drain for 30 minutes. After, crumble the tofu and set it aside.
2. Melt the vegan butter in a large pot over medium heat and sauté the onion and garlic until the veggies are fragrant and soft; 3 minutes.
3. Stir in the crumbled tofu and cook until golden brown; 3 minutes.
4. Add the butternut squash, bell pepper, paprika, red chili flakes, basil, cardamom seeds and black pepper. Cook for 2 minutes to release some flavor and mix in the tomatoes and 2 cups of vegetable broth.
5. Close the lid, bring the soup to a boil, and then simmer for 10 minutes.
6. Stir in the remaining vegetable broth and the red wine vinegar and adjust the taste with black pepper.
7. Dish the soup, garnish with the parsley and serve warm.

Nutritional Facts: Calories 320; Fat 10 g; Protein 10 g; Carbs 20 g

Red Lentil Soup

Preparation: 10 minutes   **Cooking: 25 minutes**   **Servings: 4**

INGREDIENTS

- 1 large yellow onion, diced
- 3 garlic cloves, minced
- 2 tbsp Hungarian paprika, plus more for seasoning
- 3 cups water, plus 1 tbsp
- 4 oz. tomato paste
- 1 tsp ground mustard
- 1 (14-oz.) can light coconut milk
- ¼ tsp freshly ground black pepper
- 3 carrots, diced
- 1 celery stalk, diced
- Chopped scallions, green parts only, for serving
- 1 cup dried red lentils, rinsed

DIRECTIONS

1. Combine the onion and garlic in an 8-quart saucepan over high heat. Cook for 2 to 3 minutes, adding 1 tbsp of water at a time to prevent scorching until the onion is transparent but not browned.
2. Combine the tomato paste, paprika, mustard and pepper in a mixing bowl. Cook, constantly stirring, for 2 minutes.
3. Now add the remaining 3 water cups of water and mix well. Mix the carrots and celery in a mixing bowl. Bring the broth to a boil before adding the lentils. Reduce the heat to medium-low, cover, and leave to cook for 10 minutes.
4. Stir in the coconut milk and take to a boil, stirring constantly, for almost 5 minutes, or until the lentils are cooked.
5. Top with scallions and a sprinkling of Hungarian paprika and pepper to serve.

Nutritional Facts: Calories 309; Fat 9 g; Protein 15 g; Carbohydrates 48 g; Fiber 10 g

Wild Rice Mushroom Soup

Preparation: 1 hr. 15 minutes   **Cooking: 45 minutes**   **Servings: 4**

INGREDIENTS

- ½ cup walnuts
- 4 cups no-sodium vegetable broth
- 9 oz. baby portabella mushrooms, coarsely chopped
- 1 tbsp balsamic vinegar, plus more for drizzling
- 4 oz. shiitake mushrooms, coarsely chopped
- 4 garlic cloves, minced
- ½ celery stalk, minced
- 3 thyme sprigs, divided
-
- ½ cup wild rice
- 4 cups unsweetened non-dairy milk
- ½ cup brown rice
- 1 rosemary sprig
- Freshly ground black pepper.

DIRECTIONS

1. Combine the vegetable broth and walnuts in a high-speed blender. Allow the walnuts to soften for 1 hour. You may alternatively soak the walnuts in an airtight glass jar overnight.
2. Combine the portabella and shiitake mushrooms in an 8-quart saucepan over medium-high heat. Cook for 5 minutes to allow the mushrooms to release most of their liquid. Cook for 1 minute more after adding the vinegar. Remove from the heat. Place the mushrooms in a non-plastic mixing bowl.
3. Then ¼ cup of the mushroom mixture, together with the vegetable broth and walnuts, should be blended. Pulse until the mushrooms and walnuts are completely combined. Place aside.
4. Heat the garlic, celery and 1 thyme sprig in an empty saucepan over medium-high heat. Sauté for 1 minute.
5. Return the mushrooms to the pot. Add the flour to coat the mushrooms.
6. Pour in the blended stock, followed by the milk, wild and brown rice, rosemary twig and the remaining 2 thyme sprigs. Now take the mixture to a boil, then reduce to medium-low heat, cover, and cook for 25–30 minutes, or when the rice is soft but chewy.
7. Season with pepper and a sprinkle of vinegar.

Nutritional Facts: Calories 337; Fat 12 g; Protein 12 g; Carbohydrates 51 g; Fiber 6 g

Cauliflower and Roasted Potato Soup

Preparation: 20 minutes **Cooking: 30 minutes** **Servings: 6**

INGREDIENTS

- 1 large cauliflower head, small florets cut
- 8 garlic cloves, peeled
- 2 russet potatoes, 1-inch pieces peeled and chopped
- 1 yellow onion, coarsely chopped
- 1 tbsp water, plus more as needed
- 1 celery stalk, coarsely chopped
- 6 cups no-sodium vegetable broth
- 2 tsp paprika
- 2 thyme sprigs
- 1 tbsp chopped fresh rosemary leaves
- ¼ tsp freshly ground black pepper

DIRECTIONS

1. Preheat the oven to 450°F. Line a baking sheet with parchment paper.
2. Wrap the garlic cloves in foil or place them in a garlic roaster.
3. Arrange the cauliflower and potatoes on the prepared baking sheet in an even layer. Place the garlic on the baking sheet and covered it in foil.
4. Roast the cauliflower for 15 to 20 minutes, or until it is gently browned.
5. Combine the onion and celery in an 8-quart saucepan over high heat. Cook for 4 to 5 minutes, adding 1 tbsp of water at a time to prevent burning until the onion begins to brown.
6. Bring the soup to a simmer with the vegetable broth.
7. Combine the roasted vegetables, garlic, thyme, paprika and pepper in a mixing bowl. Now take the soup to a boil, then cover and cook for 10 minutes.
8. Take out the thyme and set it aside. Puree the soup with an electric immersion blender until smooth. If the soup is too thick, add more water to get the desired consistency.
9. Add the rosemary and mix well.

Nutritional Facts: Calories 120; Fat 1 g; Protein 5 g; Carbohydrates 26 g; Fiber 5 g

Pesto Pea Soup

Preparation: 10 Minutes **Cooking: 20 Minutes** **Servings: 4**

INGREDIENTS

- 2 cups water
- 8 oz. wholemeal pasta
- ¼ cup Pesto
- 1 onion, small and finely chopped
- 1 lb. peas, frozen
- 1 carrot, medium and finely chopped
- 1 ¾ cup vegetable broth, less sodium
- 1 celery rib, medium and finely chopped

DIRECTIONS

1. To start with, boil the water in a large pot over medium-high heat.
2. Next, stir the pasta into the pot and cook it, following the instructions given in the packet.
3. In the meantime, cook the onion, celery, and carrot in a deep saucepan along with the water and broth.
4. Cook the celery-onion mixture for 6 minutes or until softened.
5. Now, spoon in the peas and allow them to simmer while keeping them uncovered.
6. Cook the peas for a few minutes or until they are bright green and soft.
7. Then, spoon the pesto into the pea mixture. Combine well.
8. Pour the mixture into a high-speed blender and blend for 2 to 3 minutes or until you get a rich, smooth soup.
9. Return the soup to the pan. Spoon in the cooked pasta.
10. Finally, pour into a serving bowl and top with more cooked peas if desired.

Nutritional Facts: Calories 100; Fat 0 g; Protein 0 g; Carbs 0 g

ENTRÉES, PASTA, RICE, PIZZA

Pizza Crust

Preparation: 10 minutes   Cooking: 20 minutes   Servings: 1

INGREDIENTS

- 3 cups broccoli rice, steamed
-
- 3 tbsp vegan Alfredo sauce
- ½ cup vegan parmesan cheese, grated

DIRECTIONS

1. Drain the broccoli rice and combine with the parmesan cheese in a bowl, mixing well.
2. Cut a piece of parchment paper roughly the size of the base of the fryer's basket. Spoon 4 equal-sized amounts of the broccoli mixture onto the paper and press each portion into the shape of a pizza crust. You may have to complete this part in 2 batches. Transfer the parchment to the fryer.
3. Cook at 370°F for five minutes. When the crust is firm, flip it over and cook for an additional 2 minutes.
4. Add the Alfredo sauce and mozzarella cheese on top of the crusts and cook for an additional 7 minutes. The crusts are ready when the sauce and cheese have melted. Serve hot.

Nutritional Facts: Calories 420; Fat 37 g; Carbs 5 g; Protein 4 g

Quinoa and Rice Stuffed Peppers (oven-baked)

Preparation: 10–30 minutes   Cooking: 35 minutes   Servings: 8

INGREDIENTS

- 3/4 cup long grain rice
- 8 bell peppers (any color)
- 2 tbsp vegetable stock
- 1 onion finely diced
- 2 cloves chopped garlic
- 1 can (11 oz) crushed tomatoes
- 1 tsp cumin
- 1 tsp coriander
- 4 tbsp ground walnuts
- 2 cups cooked quinoa
- 4 tbsp chopped parsley
- ground black pepper, to taste

DIRECTIONS

1. Preheat the oven to 400°F/200°C.
2. Boil rice and drain in a colander.
3. Cut the top stem section of the bell pepper off, remove the remaining pith and seeds, and rinse the peppers.
4. Heat vegetable stock in a large frying skillet and sauté onion and garlic until soft.
5. Add tomatoes, cumin, ground almonds, pepper and coriander; stir well and simmer for 2 minutes, stirring constantly.
6. Remove from the heat and add the rice, quinoa and parsley; stir well.
7. Taste and adjust the pepper.
8. Fill the bell peppers with a mixture, and place peppers cut side-up in a baking dish; drizzle with little vegetable stock.
9. Bake for 15 minutes.
10. Serve warm.

Nutritional Facts: Calories 335.69; Calories from Fat 83.63 g; Total Fat 9.58 g; Saturated Fat 1.2 g

Easy Vegan Pizza Bread

Preparation: 5 minutes   **Cooking: 20 minutes**   **Servings: 4**

INGREDIENTS

- 1 wholewheat loaf, unsliced
- 1 cup Easy One-Pot Vegan Marinara
- 1 tsp nutritional yeast
- ½ tsp onion powder
- ½ tsp garlic powder

DIRECTIONS

1. Preheat the oven to 375°F.
2. Halve the loaf of bread lengthwise. Evenly spread the marinara onto each slice of bread, then sprinkle on the nutritional yeast, onion powder and garlic powder.
3. Place the bread on a baking sheet and bake for 20 minutes, or until the bread is a light golden brown.

Ingredient Tip: If you're having a tough time finding a good wholewheat loaf, or if you'd just prefer a thinner crust, you can easily substitute a tortilla shell or pita (here) for the loaf of bread.

Nutritional Facts: Calories 230; Total fat 3 g; Carbohydrates 38 g; Fiber 7 g; Protein 13 g

Sweet Potato Gnocchi

Preparation: 50 minutes   **Cooking: 1 hr. 20 minutes**   **Servings: 2**

INGREDIENTS

- 1 large sweet potato
- ¾ cup whole-wheat flour, plus more for the work surface
- 4 quarts water, plus 1 tbsp
- 3 garlic cloves, minced
- 2 handfuls fresh spinach

DIRECTIONS

1. Poke holes in the skin of the sweet potato with a fork or the tip of a knife. Microwave for 10 minutes on high power with the skin on, or bake for 1 hour at 350°F. The sweet potato flesh should be tender.
2. Cut the potato in half lengthwise. Then scoop the flesh out into a basin. Using a fork, mash the potatoes well. Mix in the flour with a fork to blend.
3. Dust a work surface lightly with flour and place the dough on it. Knead the dough for 2 to 3 minutes. Roll the dough into a ½-inch-thick rope.
4. Cut the rope into ¼-inch lengths. To make grooves, lightly rub the tines of a fork across each piece.
5. Bring 4 quarts of water to a boil in a large pot over high heat. Reduce the heat so that the water is kept at a simmer and carefully place the gnocchi in it. Cook for about 2 minutes, or until they float to the surface.
6. 1 tbsp water, heated in a medium pan over medium-high heat. Cook for 1 minute after adding the garlic. Cook, stirring constantly, until the spinach wilts. Cook, stirring constantly, for 1 minute more after adding the cooked gnocchi. Remove from the heat and serve.

Nutritional Facts: Calories 258; Fat 2 g; Protein 9 g; Carbohydrates 55 g; Fiber 8 g

Color Pasta

Preparation: 10 minutes   **Cooking: 10 minutes**   **Servings: 1**

INGREDIENTS

- 1 medium carrot
- 1 small-medium zucchini
- 2 oz. wholewheat spaghetti
- 1/3–½ cup tomato sauce
- 3 tbsp sundried tomato spread
- vegan parmesan cheese
- fresh basil

DIRECTIONS

1. Start by cooking the noodles as per the given instructions on the box until al dente.
2. Pass the zucchini and carrot through a spiralizer to get the noodles.
3. Heat the tomato sauce in a pan.
4. Boil the carrot and zucchini noodles in the pasta water for 4 minutes until al dente.
5. Drain and toss the vegetables with cooked pasta noodles and tomato mixture in a bowl.
6. Garnish as desired.
7. Serve.

Nutrition Facts: Calories 341; Total Fat 4 g; Saturated Fat 0.5 g; Cholesterol 69 mg; Sodium 547 mg; Total Carbs 36.4 g; Fiber 1.2 g; Protein 10.3 g

Baked Mac and Peas

Preparation: 15 minutes   **Cooking: 40 minutes**   **Servings: 8**

INGREDIENTS

- 1 (16-oz.) package whole-wheat macaroni pasta
- 1 jar vegan "Cheese" Sauce
- 2 cups green peas (fresh or frozen)

DIRECTIONS

1. Preheat the oven to 400°F.
2. In a large stockpot, cook the pasta per the package instructions for al dente. Drain the pasta.
3. Combine the pasta, sauce and peas in a large baking dish, and mix well.
4. Bake for 30 minutes or until the top of the dish turns golden brown.

Cooking Tip: If you'd prefer not to bake this recipe, it can always be prepared, like a portion of traditional macaroni and cheese. All you need to do is boil your noodles according to the package directions and then drain the water before stirring in the cheese sauce.

Nutritional Facts: Calories 209; Total fat 3 g; Carbohydrates 42 g; Fiber 7 g; Protein 12 g

One Pan Spicy Rice

Preparation: 5 Minutes   **Cooking: 25 Minutes**   **Servings: 5**

INGREDIENTS

- non-dairy yogurt, to serve
- 2 cups spinach
- 1 handful raisins
- 15 oz. chickpeas, rinsed and drained
- 2 cups vegetable stock
- 1½ cups basmati rice, rinsed
- 2 tbsp curry paste
- 9 crushed garlic cloves
- 1 tbsp vegetable stock

DIRECTIONS

1. Take out a pan and heat some vegetable stock inside. When it is hot, you can add the curry paste and garlic to cook and heat up for a minute.
2. When this is done, add the pepper, chickpeas, raisins, vegetable stock and rice into the pan, and stir it around well.
3. Reduce the heat for a bit and let this cook. After 15 minutes, all the liquid should be gone, and the rice should be tender. Add the spinach as well.
4. Serve with some of the natural yogurts and enjoy it.

Nutritional Facts: Calories 170; Carbs 16 g; Fat 2 g; Protein 5 g

Pesto Quinoa with White Beans

Preparation: 5 minutes   **Cooking: 15 minutes**   **Servings: 4**

INGREDIENTS

- 12 oz. cooked white bean
- 3 ½ cups quinoa, cooked
- 1 medium zucchini, sliced For the Pesto:
- 1/3 cup walnuts
- 2 cups arugula
- 1 tsp minced garlic
- 2 cups basil
- ¾ tsp cilantro
- ¼ tsp ground black pepper
- 1 tbsp lemon juice
- 1/3 cup vegetable stock
- 2 tbsp water
- ¾ cup sun-dried tomato
- ¼ cup pine nuts
- 1 tbsp vegetable stock

DIRECTIONS

1. Prepare the pesto, and for this, place all of its ingredients in a food processor and pulse for 2 minutes until smooth, scraping the sides of the container frequently, setting aside until required.
2. Take a large skillet pan, place it over medium heat, add vegetable stock and when hot, add the zucchini and cook for 4 minutes until tender-crisp.
3. Season the zucchini with cilantro and black pepper, cook for 2 minutes until lightly brown, then add the tomatoes and white beans, and continue cooking for 4 minutes until the white beans begin to crisp.
4. Stir in pine nuts, cook for 2 minutes until toasted, remove the pan from heat, and transfer the zucchini mixture into a medium bowl.
5. Add quinoa and pesto, stir until well combined, distribute among four bowls, and serve.

Nutritional Facts: Calories 352; Saturated Fat 5 g; Carbohydrates 33.7 g; Protein 9.7 g;

Brown Rice and Vegetable Stir-Fry

Preparation: 5 minutes	Cooking: 50 minutes	Servings: 4

INGREDIENTS

- 16-oz. tofu, extra-firm, pressed, drained, cut into ½-inch cubes
- 1 cup brown rice
- 1 cup frozen broccoli florets
- 1 medium red bell pepper, cored, diced
- 1 small white onion, peeled, diced
- 1 tbsp minced garlic
- ½ tsp cilantro
- 1/3 tsp ground black pepper
- 1 tbsp vegetable stock
- 2 cups vegetable broth

DIRECTIONS

1. Take a medium pot, place it over high heat, add brown rice, pour in vegetable broth, and bring it to a boil.
2. Switch heat to medium-low level, cover the pot with the lid and cook for 40 minutes, and when done, remove the pot and set aside until required.
3. Then, take a large skillet pan, place it over medium-high heat, add vegetable stock and when hot, add tofu pieces, onion, broccoli and bell pepper; season with cilantro and black pepper and cook for 5 minutes until sauté.
4. Add cooked rice, stir until mixed, and continue cooking for 5 minutes.
5. Serve straight away.

Nutritional Facts: Calories 281.9; Fat 11.7 g; Saturated Fat 1.7 g; Carbohydrates 31.1 g; Fiber 9.7 g; Protein 20.1 g

Tomato Basil Spaghetti

Preparation: 5 minutes	Cooking: 20 minutes	Servings: 4

INGREDIENTS

- 15-oz. cooked great northern beans
- 10.5-oz. cherry tomatoes halved
- 1 small white onion, peeled, diced
- 1 tbsp minced garlic
- 8 basil leaves, chopped
- 2 tbsp vegetable stock
- 1-pound spaghetti

DIRECTIONS

1. Take a large pot half full with water, place it over medium-high heat, bring it to a boil, add the spaghetti, and cook for 10 to 12 minutes until tender.
2. Then, drain the spaghetti with a colander and reserve 1 cup of pasta liquid.
3. Take a large skillet pan, place it over medium-high heat, add vegetable stock and when hot, add onion, tomatoes, basil and garlic, and cook for 5 minutes until vegetables have turned tender.
4. Add cooked spaghetti and beans, pour in pasta water, stir until mixed, and cook for 2 minutes until hot.
5. Serve immediately.

Nutritional Facts: Calories 147; Fat 5 g; Saturated Fat 0.7 g; Carbohydrates 21.2 g; Fiber 1.5 g

Bean and Rice Burritos

Preparation: 10 minutes   **Cooking: 20 minutes**   **Servings: 6**

INGREDIENTS

- 32 oz. refried beans
- 2 cups cooked rice
- 2 cups chopped spinach
- 1 tbsp vegetable stock
- ½ cup tomato salsa
- 6 tortillas, whole grain, warm
- Guacamole as needed for serving

DIRECTIONS

1. Switch on the oven, set it to 375°F and let it preheat.
2. Take a medium saucepan, place it over medium heat, add the beans, and cook for 3 to 5 minutes until softened; remove the pan from the heat.
3. Place one tortilla on a clean working space, spread some of the beans on it into a log, leaving 2-inches off the edge, top beans with spinach, rice and salsa, and then tightly wrap the tortilla to seal the filling like a burrito.
4. Repeat with the remaining tortillas, place these burritos on a baking sheet, brush them with vegetable stock, and then bake for 15 minutes until golden.
5. Serve the burritos with guacamole.

Nutritional Facts: Calories 421; Fat 9 g; Saturated Fat 2 g; Carbohydrates 70 g; Fiber 11 g; Protein 15 g

SIDES

Easy Portobello Mushrooms

Preparation: 10 minutes   Cooking: 10 minutes   Servings: 4

INGREDIENTS

- 12 cherry tomatoes
- 2 oz. scallions
- 4 Portobello mushrooms
- 4 and ¼ oz. almond butter
- Sunflower seeds and pepper, to taste

DIRECTIONS

1. Take a large skillet and melt the almond butter over medium heat
2. Add the mushrooms and sauté for 3 minutes
3. Stir in cherry tomatoes and scallions
4. Sauté for 5 minutes
5. Season accordingly
6. Sauté until the vegetables are tender
7. Enjoy!

Nutritional Facts: Calories 154; Fat 10 g; Carbohydrates 2 g; Protein 7 g

Broccoli Puree

Preparation: 15 minutes   Cooking: 15 minutes   Servings: 6

INGREDIENTS

- 1 pound broccoli florets
- 1/3 cup almond milk
- 1 cup water
- 1 tsp dried oregano
- ½ tsp coriander, ground

DIRECTIONS

1. Put the broccoli and the water in the instant pot and close the lid.
2. Cook for 15 minutes on manual mode (high pressure). Use natural pressure release for 10 minutes.
3. Strain, transfer to the food processor, add the rest of the ingredients, and pulse.
4. Divide it among plates and serve.

Nutritional Facts: Calories 182; Fat 3.8 g; Fiber 4.8 g; Carbs 11.1 g; Protein 2 g

Spaghetti Squash and Leeks

Preparation: 15 minutes   Cooking: 10 minutes   Servings: 4

INGREDIENTS

- 2 leeks, sliced
- 1 tsp chili powder
- 1 tsp cumin, ground
- 1 tsp onion powder
- 1 tsp apple cider vinegar
- 1-pound spaghetti squash, halved, seeds removed
- 1 tbsp Italian seasoning
- 1 cup water, for cooking

DIRECTIONS

1. Pour water into the instant pot and insert the steamer rack.
2. Arrange spaghetti squash on the rack and close the lid.
3. Cook it on High for 10 minutes. Then allow natural pressure release for 5 minutes.
4. Check if the spaghetti squash is soft, shred the flesh with the help of a fork, and transfer to a bowl.
5. Add the rest of the ingredients, toss, and serve.

Nutritional Facts: Calories 110; Fat 1.7 g; Fiber 0 g; Carbs 4.3 g; Protein 0.8 g

Paprika Sweet Potato

Preparation: 10 minutes   **Cooking: 11 minutes**   **Servings: 2**

INGREDIENTS

- 2 sweet potatoes
- 2 tsp sweet paprika
- ½ tsp oregano, dried
- 1 tsp chili powder
- 1 tsp chives, chopped
- ½ cup water

DIRECTIONS

1. Pour water into the instant pot and insert the steamer rack.
2. Put the potatoes on the rack and close the lid.
3. Set Manual mode (High pressure) and cook for 11 minutes. Then use quick pressure release.
4. Transfer the potatoes to the plate, cut them into halves, sprinkle the rest of the ingredients on top, and serve.

Nutritional Facts: Calories 159; Fat 3.4 g; Fiber 2.8 g; Carbs 33.8 g; Protein 3.6 g

Cinnamon Carrots

Preparation: 10 minutes   **Cooking: 15 minutes**   **Servings: 4**

INGREDIENTS

- 1 pound baby carrots, scrubbed
- 1/3 cup water
- 1 tsp ground cinnamon
- ¼ tsp chili powder
- 1 tsp black pepper

DIRECTIONS

1. In the instant pot, mix the carrots with the water and the other ingredients, close the lid, and in Manual mode (High pressure) for 15 minutes.
2. After this, use the quick pressure release.
3. Divide it among plates and serve.

Nutritional Facts: Calories 147; Fat 0.5 g; Fiber 7.1 g; Carbs 9.9 g; Protein 4.3 g

Oven Potato Fries

Preparation: 15 minutes   **Cooking: 30 minutes**   **Servings: 1**

INGREDIENTS

- 2 ½ pounds baking potatoes
- 1 tsp avocado puree
- 1 pinch ground cayenne pepper

DIRECTIONS

1. Start by preheating the oven by setting the temperature to 450°F. Take a baking sheet and line it with foil. Spray the sheet with a generous amount of cooking spray.
2. Scrub well to clean the potatoes. Cut each potato into half an inch-thick strips.
3. Take a large-sized mixing bowl and toss in the potato strips. Add in the avocado puree and cayenne pepper.
4. Place the coated fries on the baking tray lined with cooking spray. Place the baking sheet in the preheated oven and bake for about 30 minutes. Transfer onto a serving platter and serve right away.

Nutritional Facts: Calories 263; Carbs 35 g; Fat 12 g; Protein 4 g

Mushrooms with Herbs and White Wine

Preparation: 10 minutes   **Cooking: 15 minutes**   **Servings: 1**

INGREDIENTS

- 2 tbsp vegetable stock
- 1 ½ pound fresh mushrooms
- 1 tsp Italian seasoning
- ¼ cup dry white wine
- 2 cloves garlic (minced)
- garlic powder, as per taste
- pepper, as per taste
- 2 tbsp fresh chives (chopped)

DIRECTIONS

1. Start by heating the vegetable stock by placing the nonstick skillet on medium-high flame. Once the vegetable stock is heated, toss in the mushrooms. Sprinkle the Italian seasoning and sauté for about 10 minutes. Keep stirring.
2. Pour in the dry white wine and toss in the garlic. Continue to cook for about 3–4 minutes. Season with pepper and garlic powder. Sprinkle the chives and cook for about a minute. Move into a serving bowl, then serve hot.

Nutritional Facts: Calories 522; Carbs 27 g; Fat 16 g; Protein 55 g

Zucchini Stuffed with Mushrooms and Chickpeas

Preparation: 30 minutes   **Cooking: 30 minutes**   **Servings: 1**

INGREDIENTS

- 4 zucchinis (halved)
- 2 tbsp vegetable stock
- 1 onion (chopped)
- 2 cloves garlic (crushed)
- ½ package button mushrooms, sliced (8 oz.)
- 1 tsp ground coriander
- 1 ½ tsp ground cumin
- 1 can chickpeas (15.5 oz.)
- ½ lemon (juiced)
- 2 tbsp fresh parsley (chopped)
- garlic powder, as per taste
- ground black pepper, as per taste

DIRECTIONS

1. Start by preheating the oven by setting the temperature to 350°F. Take a shallow non-stick baking dish and grease it generously.
2. Using a spoon, scoop out the flesh in the center of the zucchini halves. Chop the flesh into the zucchini halves into the greased baking dish.
3. In the meanwhile, take a large non-stick skillet and place it over medium flame, and put the vegetable stock. Toss in the onions and sauté for about 5 minutes. Add in the garlic and sauté for 2 more minutes.
4. Now, add in the mushrooms and zucchini. Keep stirring and cook for about 5 minutes.
5. Add in the chickpeas, cumin, coriander, parsley, lemon juice, pepper and garlic powder. Mix well to combine.
6. Put the zucchini shells on your baking sheet and fill them with the chickpea mixture. Put the baking sheet in your oven and bake for about 40 minutes.
7. Once done, remove from the oven and transfer onto a serving platter. Serve hot!

Nutritional Facts: Calories 149; Carbs 10 g; Fat 10 g; Protein 8 g

Vegan Onion Rings

Preparation: 30 minutes	Cooking: 10 minutes	Servings: 4 servings

INGREDIENTS

- 2 sweet onions, peeled
- 2/3 cup buckwheat flour
- 2/3 cup almond milk, unsweetened
- 1 tsp garlic powder
- 1 tsp smoked paprika powder
- 1 tbsp nutritional yeast
- 1 cup panko breadcrumbs

DIRECTIONS

1. Preheat the oven to 350°F. Line a baking sheet with parchment paper. Combine flour, spices, nutritional yeast and almond milk in a bowl. Stir well.
2. Place the breadcrumbs into a separate bowl. Cut the onions into ¼ inch rings and separate.
3. Coat each onion ring in the spices, then follow by dipping it in the breadcrumbs. Lay the onion rings onto the baking sheet when finished.
4. Bake for 20 minutes. Remove the pan and flip each onion ring. Bake for an additional 10 minutes. Serve warm with additional dipping sauce if desired.

Nutritional Facts: Calories 200; Fat 1 g; Protein 6 g; Carbs 40 g

Korean Braised Tofu

Preparation: 15 minutes	Cooking: 5 minutes	Servings: 4

INGREDIENTS

- 14 oz. block firm tofu, cut into 16 squares
- 1 tbsp brown rice syrup
- 1 scallion, thinly cut
- 1 onion, thinly cut
- 3 tbsp soy sauce
- 1 tbsp Korean chili powder
- 4 tbsp sake
- Sesame seeds, toasted as desired

DIRECTIONS

1. Add onion slices to a pan and add tofu on top. Mix soy sauce, Korean chili powder, sake and brown rice syrup in a bowl and add over tofu slices.
2. Cover the pan. Increase the heat to high and cook until it boils. Turn the heat to medium-high and cook for 5 minutes, baste with sauce.
3. Remove the lid, raise the heat to high, and then cook until the sauce reduces. Transfer to a plate, garnish with sesame seeds and serve.

Nutritional Facts: Calories 160; Carbs 14 g; Fat 8 g; Protein 10 g

SALADS

Artichoke Tofu Salad

Preparation: 10 minutes   Cooking: 35 minutes   Servings: 4

INGREDIENTS

- 2 (14-oz.) cans quartered artichoke hearts, drained
- 1 block of Tofu
- ½ cup Tofu Sour Cream
- ½ cup diced sweet onion
- ½ cup diced celery
- 1 tsp dulse flakes, or 1 tsp Spicy Umami Blend

DIRECTIONS

1. Coarsely chop the artichoke hearts and transfer them to a medium bowl.
2. Add the sour cream, onion, celery, tofu and dulse, and stir to combine.
3. Move the mixture to a sealed container and refrigerate for at least 30 minutes before serving.

Nutritional Facts: Calories 157; Fats 3 g; Protein 10 g; Carbohydrates 27 g

The Waldorf Salad

Preparation: 15 minutes   Cooking: 10 minutes   Servings: 4

INGREDIENTS

- ½ cup Tofu Sour Cream
- 3 tbsp lemon juice
- 2 tbsp nutritional yeast
- 2 garlic cloves, minced
- 1 Medjool date, pitted (optional)
- ½ cup chopped walnuts
- Zest 1 lemon (optional)
- 2 large Honeycrisp or Gala apples, cored and cut into ¼-inch pieces
- 2 celery stalks, chop into ½-inch pieces
- 1 cup grapes (any kind), halved
- 1 head red-leaf lettuce, chopped or torn into bite-size pieces
- 1 head Bibb or Boston lettuce, chopped or torn into bite-size pieces

DIRECTIONS

1. With a food processor or blender, mix in the sour cream, lemon juice, nutritional yeast, garlic and date. Purée until creamy and pourable.
2. If needed, put in 2 tbsp of water to make it thinner. Set aside.
3. In a small bowl, combine the walnuts and lemon zest (if used).
4. Get a large bowl combining the apples, celery and grapes. Add the lettuces and toss to combine. Add the dressing on the salad and toss until evenly coated.
5. Portion the salad into 4 bowls. Sprinkle 2 tbsp of the walnut-lemon zest mixture over each salad and serve.

Nutritional Facts: Calories 255; Fats 12 g; Protein 9 g; Carbohydrates 34 g

Chickpea Pecan Salad

Preparation: 10 minutes   Cooking: 5 minutes   Servings: 4

INGREDIENTS

- 1 (15-oz.) can chickpeas, drained and rinsed
- 1 (4-oz.) jar hearts palm, drained
- ½ tsp ground thyme
- ½ tsp ground sage
- 1 large celery stalk, chopped
- ¼ cup dried cranberries
- 2 tbsp rice vinegar
- ¼ cup chopped pecans

DIRECTIONS

1. Add in chickpeas and hearts of palm in a food processor, and pulse in 1-second bursts until the mixture has a flaky texture. Be careful not to over-process.
2. Transfer the mixture to a medium bowl.
3. Add the thyme, sage, celery, cranberries, vinegar and pecans, and stir to combine.
4. Serve immediately.

Nutritional Facts: Calories: 225; Fats 7 g; Protein 8 g; Carbohydrates 35 g

Classic Wedge Salad

Preparation: 15 minutes   **Cooking: 15 minutes**   **Servings: 4**

INGREDIENTS

- 2 carrots, finely diced
- 2 tbsp low-sodium soy sauce or tamari
- 2 tsp pure agave syrup
- ½ tsp smoked paprika
- 2 ripe avocados
- 2 tbsp apple cider vinegar
- 1 tbsp nutritional yeast
- 1 tsp spirulina powder (optional)
- 1 small red onion, sliced
- 1 cup cherry or grape tomatoes, halved
- 1 head iceberg lettuce, cut into 4 wedges
- freshly ground black pepper

DIRECTIONS

1. Prepare carrots in a small bowl and let sit for 10 minutes.
2. Whisk the soy sauce, agave syrup and paprika, then pour it over the carrots. Set aside.
3. Remove the avocado pits by slicing them in half. Dice the flesh of one of the avocado halves in the peel, then gently scoop it out into a small bowl. Set aside.
4. Scoop the flesh from the 3 remaining avocado halves into a blender.
5. Add the vinegar, nutritional yeast and spirulina (if used), and purée until smooth, creamy, and pourable.
6. Put more water if needed to reach the right consistency. Pour the dressing into a medium bowl.
7. Add the onion, tomatoes and carrots (along with the liquid in the bowl) to the bowl.
8. Pour the dressing and stir to combine. Gently fold the diced avocado into the dressing.
9. Place a wedge of lettuce on each of the 4 salad plates. Dress the lettuce by spooning about ½ cup of dressing over each wedge, then repeat until the dressing is used up.
10. Sprinkle with black pepper over each salad and serve.

Nutritional Facts: Calories: 298; Fats 20 g; Protein 8 g; Carbohydrates 29 g

Jackfruit Louie Avocado Salad

Preparation: 10 minutes   **Cooking: 10 minutes**   **Servings: 4**

INGREDIENTS

- ½ cup Tofu Sour Cream
- 2 tsp apple cider vinegar
- 1 garlic clove, minced
- ¼ tsp ground ginger
- ¼ tsp ground mustard
- ¼ tsp onion powder
- 1 (14-oz.) can jackfruit, drained
- 1 tsp chili powder
- 8 cups chopped lettuce
- 2 ripe avocados, halved and pitted

DIRECTIONS

1. Get a small bowl, then mix together the sour cream, vinegar, garlic, ginger, ground mustard and onion powder. Set aside.
2. Place the jackfruit in a medium bowl. Dust with the chili powder and stir until evenly coated. Stir in the sour cream mixture to combine. Set aside.
3. Plate 2 cups of the chopped lettuce on each of the 4 salad plates. Scoop the flesh from 1 avocado half over the lettuce on each plate.
4. Spoon ½ cup of the jackfruit mixture into each avocado half. Spoon the remaining jackfruit mixture equally over each plate and serve.

Nutritional Facts: Calories 337; Fats 18 g; Protein 11 g; Carbohydrates 39 g

Potato in Creamy Avocado Salad

Preparation: 10 minutes   **Cooking: 1 hour**   **Servings: 4**

INGREDIENTS

- 5 large potatoes, cut into 1-inch cubes
- 1 large avocado, chopped
- ¼ cup chopped fresh chives
- ½ tbsp freshly squeezed lemon juice
- 2 tbsp no honey Dijon mustard
- ½ tsp onion powder
- ½ tsp garlic powder
- ½ tsp dried dill
- ¼ tsp freshly ground black pepper

DIRECTIONS

1. Place the potatoes in a pot, then pour in enough water to cover. Bring to a boil for 10 more minutes or until the potatoes are soft.
2. Let the potatoes cool for 10 minutes, then put the potatoes in a colander and rinse under running water.
3. Dry potatoes with paper towels and transfer to a large bowl. Refrigerate for at least 20 minutes.
4. Meanwhile, combine the avocado with chives, lemon juice and mustard in a food processor. Sprinkle onion powder, garlic powder, dill and pepper. Pulse to mash the avocado until creamy and well combined.
5. Pour the creamy avocado into the bowl of potatoes, then toss to coat the potato cubes well. Refrigerate for 30 minutes before serving.

Nutritional Facts: Calories 242; Fat 9 g; Carbohydrates 35 g; Protein 7 g

Fresh Citrus Salad with Orange and Grapefruit

Preparation: 10 minutes   **Cooking: 10 minutes**   **Servings: 2**

INGREDIENTS

- 1 large grapefruit, peeled, pith removed and segmented
- 2 large oranges, peeled, pith removed, and segmented
- zest and juice of 1 lime
- 1 tsp pure agave syrup (optional)
- 1 tbsp minced fresh mint

DIRECTIONS

1. Combine all the ingredients in a mixing bowl apart from the fresh mint and mix until well coated.
2. Transfer the salad to the serving dishes and add the fresh mint on top.
3. Serve immediately.

Nutritional Facts: Calories 154; Fat 0.4 g; Carbohydrates 39.2 g; Protein 2.9 g

Rice, Chickpea, Fennel, and Orange Salad

Preparation: 15 minutes   **Cooking: 1 hour and 50 minutes**   **Servings: 4**

INGREDIENTS

- 1 ½ cup brown basmati, rinsed
- 3 cups water
- 2 cups chickpeas, soaked in water overnight, cooked
- 1 fennel bulb, trimmed and diced
- zest and segments 1 orange
- ¼ cup parsley, finely chopped
- ¼ cup white wine vinegar, and 2 tbsp additional
- ½ tsp red pepper flakes

DIRECTIONS

1. Put the soaked chickpeas in a saucepan, then pour in the water to cover by about 1 inch.
2. Bring to a boil over medium-high heat. Adjust the heat to low and simmer for 60 minutes or until soft. Allow cooling before using.
3. Put the brown basmati in a pot, then pour in the water.
4. Bring to a boil over high heat. Change heat to medium, then simmer for 45 to 50 minutes or until the water is absorbed.
5. Combine the cooked basmati with the remaining ingredients in a large serving bowl. Toss to combine well, then serve immediately.

Nutritional Facts: Calories 438; Fat 4.4 g; Carbohydrates 86.3 g; Protein 14.1 g

Lemony Millet and Fruit Salad

Preparation: 10 minutes   **Cooking: 15 minutes**   **Servings: 4**

INGREDIENTS

DRESSING:

- 3 tbsp agave syrup
- juice 1 lemon
- zest and juice 1 orange

SALAD:

- 1 cup cooked millet
- ½ cup golden raisins
- ½ cup dried currants
- ½ cup dried unsulfured apricots, chopped
- 1 Gala apple, cored and diced
- 2 tbsp finely chopped mint

DIRECTIONS

1. Put the rinsed millet in a pot, then pour in the water to cover it by about 1 inch. Bring to a boil over high heat.
2. Change the heat to medium and keep boiling for 12 to 14 minutes or until tender. Allow cooling before using.
3. For the dressing: Prepare and combine all the ingredients in a large bowl. Stir to mix well.
4. Add the ingredients for the salad to the dressing and toss to combine well.
5. Refrigerate for half an hour and serve.

Nutritional Facts: Calories 328; Fat 2.4 g; Carbohydrates 72.6 g; Protein 6.8 g

Endive and Green Lentil Salad

Preparation: 10 minutes   **Cooking: 10 minutes**   **Servings: 2**

INGREDIENTS

- ½ cup chopped fresh endive, rinsed
- 2 cups cooked green lentils
- ¼ cup lemon juice
- 2 tbsp dried oregano
- 1 tbsp ground black pepper

DIRECTIONS

1. Prepare a larger serving bowl, then combine all the ingredients.
2. Toss to combine well, then serve immediately.

Nutritional Facts: Calories 261; Fat 1.2 g; Carbohydrates 48.3 g; Protein 19.0 g

Taco Tempeh Salad

Preparation: 25 minutes   **Cooking: 0 minutes**   **Servings: 3**

INGREDIENTS

- 1 cup dry black beans
- 1 8-oz. package tempeh
- 1 tbsp lime or lemon juice
- 2 tbsp avocado oil
- 1 tsp agave syrup
- ½ tsp chili powder
- ¼ tsp cumin
- ¼ tsp paprika
- 1 large bunch kale, fresh or frozen, chopped
- 1 large avocado, peeled, pitted, diced
- ½ cup salsa
- ¼ tsp pepper

DIRECTIONS

1. Prepare the beans according to the method.
2. Cut the tempeh into ¼-inch cubes, place in a bowl, and then add the lime or lemon juice, 1 tbsp of oil, agave syrup, chili powder, cumin and paprika.
3. Stir well and let the tempeh marinate in the fridge for at least 1 hour, up to 12 hours.
4. Heat the remaining 1 tbsp of avocado oil in a frying pan over medium heat.
5. Add the marinated tempeh mixture and cook until brown and crispy on both sides, around 10 minutes.
6. Put the chopped kale in a bowl with the cooked beans and prepared tempeh.
7. Store or serve the salad immediately, topped with salsa, avocado, and pepper to taste.

Nutritional Facts: Calories 585; Total Fat 25.48 g; Saturated Fat 4.22 g; Cholesterol 0 mg; Sodium 350 mg; Total Carbohydrate 63.8 g; Dietary Fiber 17.6 g; Total; Protein 35.34 g; Vitamin D 0 mcg; Calcium 343 mg; Iron 7.4 mg; Potassium 2122 mg

Lebanese Potato Salad

Preparation: 5 minutes   **Cooking: 10 minutes**   **Servings: 4**

INGREDIENTS

- 1-pound Russet potatoes
- 1½ tbsp avocado oil
- 2 scallions, thinly sliced
- Freshly ground pepper, to taste
- 2 tbsp lemon juice
- 2 tbsp fresh mint leaves, chopped

DIRECTIONS

1. Place a saucepan half-filled with water over medium heat. Add the potatoes and cook for 10 minutes until tender. Drain the potatoes and place them in a bowl of cold water. When cool enough to handle, peel and cube the potatoes. Place in a bowl.

TO MAKE THE DRESSING:

2. Add oil, lemon juice and pepper to a bowl, and whisk well. Drizzle dressing over the potatoes. Toss well.
3. Add scallions and mint, and toss well.
4. Divide into 4 plates and serve.

Nutritional Facts: Calories 113; Total Fat 5.25 g; Saturated Fat 0.6 g; Cholesterol 0 mg; Sodium 16.22 mg; Total Carbohydrate 15.77 g; Dietary Fiber 2.5 g; Protein 1.7 g; Vitamin D 0 mcg; Calcium 16.8 mg; Iron 0.66 mg; Potassium 409.56 mg

Chickpea and Spinach Salad

Preparation: 5 minutes   **Cooking: 0 minutes**   **Servings: 4**

INGREDIENTS

- 2 cans (14.5 oz. each) chickpeas, drained, rinsed
- 7 oz. vegan feta cheese, crumbled or chopped
- 1 tbsp lemon juice
- 1/3–½ cup avocado oil
- 4–6 cups spinach, torn
- ½ cup raisins
- 2 tbsp agave syrup
- 1–2 tsp ground cumin
- 1 tsp chili flakes

DIRECTIONS

1. Add cheese, chickpeas and spinach into a large bowl.
2. To make the dressing: Add the rest of the ingredients into another bowl and mix well.
3. Pour the dressing over the salad then toss it well and serve.

Nutritional Facts: Calories 600.26; Total Fat 36.34 g; Saturated Fat 14.8 g; Cholesterol 0 mg; Sodium 683 mg; Total Carbohydrate 59.9 g; Dietary Fiber 9.88 g; Protein 10.78 g; Vitamin D 0 mcg; Calcium 103 mg; Iron 2.9 mg; Potassium 498 mg

Spinach and Dill Pasta Salad

Preparation: 5 minutes   **Cooking: 0 minutes**   **Servings: 4**

INGREDIENTS

FOR SALAD:

- 3 cups cooked wholewheat fusilli
- 2 cups cherry tomatoes, halved
- ½ cup vegan cheese, shredded
- 4 cups spinach, chopped
- 2 cups edamame, thawed
- 1 large red onion, finely chopped

FOR DRESSING:

- 2 tbsp white wine vinegar
- ½ tsp dried dill
- 2 tbsp avocado oil
- Pepper, to taste

DIRECTIONS

TO MAKE THE DRESSING:

1. Add all the ingredients for the dressing into a bowl and whisk well. Set aside so that the flavors can set in.

TO MAKE THE SALAD:

2. Add all the ingredients of the salad to a bowl. Toss well.
3. Drizzle the dressing on top. Toss well.
4. Divide into 4 plates and serve.

Nutritional Facts: Calories 302.35; Total Fat 14.11 g; Saturated Fat 3.4 g; Cholesterol 0.6 mg; Sodium 95 mg; Total Carbohydrate 34.24 g; Dietary Fiber 7.79 g; Protein 13.8 g; Vitamin D 0 mcg; Calcium 94 mg; Iron 3.7 mg; Potassium 768 mg

Italian Veggie Salad

Preparation: 10 minutes   **Cooking: 0 minutes**   **Servings: 8**

INGREDIENTS

FOR SALAD:

- 1 cup fresh baby carrots, quartered lengthwise
- 1 celery rib, sliced
- 3 large mushrooms, thinly sliced
- 1 cup cauliflower florets, bite-sized, blanched
- 1 cup broccoli florets, blanched
- 1 cup thinly sliced radish
- 4–5 oz.' hearts of romaine salad mix to serve

FOR DRESSING:

- ½ package Italian salad dressing mix
- 3 tbsp white vinegar
- 3 tbsp water
- 3 tbsp avocado oil
- 3–4 pepperoncini, chopped

DIRECTIONS

TO MAKE THE SALAD:

1. Add all the ingredients of the salad except the romaine hearts to a bowl and toss.

TO MAKE THE DRESSING:

2. Add all the ingredients of the dressing to a small bowl. Whisk well.
3. Pour the dressing over salad and toss well. Refrigerate for a couple of hours.
4. Place the romaine in a large bowl. Place the chilled salad over it and serve.

Nutritional Facts: Calories 84; Total Fat 6.7 g; Saturated Fat 1.2 g; Cholesterol 3 mg; Sodium 212 mg; Total Carbohydrate 5 g; Dietary Fiber 1.4 g; Protein 2 g; Vitamin D 31 mcg; Calcium 27 mg; Iron 1 mg; Potassium 193 mg

Crusty Corn on the Cob

Preparation: 10 minutes   **Cooking: 15 minutes**   **Servings: 2**

INGREDIENTS

- 2 corn on the cob
- 1/3 cup Veganize
- 1 tbs cilantro
-
- ¼ cup of vegan Parmesan cheese
- 1 tsp lime juice

DIRECTIONS

1. Preheat the grill.
2. Add corn on the cob to the grill and continue grilling while turning until all sides are golden-brown.
3. Mix the Veganize, cilantro, breadcrumbs, vegan Parmesan, and lime juice on a plate.
4. Roll the grilled corn cobs in the crumb mixture.
5. Toss well, then serve.

Nutritional Facts: Calories 253; Total Fat 13 g; Protein 31 g; Total Carbs 3 g; Fiber 0 g; Net Carbs 3 g

Grilled Herb Carrots with Creamy Chickpea Salad

Preparation: 10 minutes   **Cooking: 10 minutes**   **Servings: 8**

INGREDIENTS

- 8 large carrots
- 1 tsp dried thyme
- 1 tsp dried oregano
- ½ tsp garlic powder
- 2 tsp paprika powder
- 1 ½ tbsp soy sauce or tamari
- ½ cup water

CHICKPEA SALAD

- 12 oz. canned chickpeas
- ½ cup vegan cream
- 2 large pickles
- 1 small onion
- ½ cup of lettuce
- 1 ½ tsp apple cider vinegar
- ½ tsp dried oregano
- ground black pepper, to taste

DIRECTIONS

1. Coat the carrots with all of their ingredients in a bowl.
2. Put a stick through each carrot and place them on a plate.
3. Preheat the grill.
4. Grill the carrots for 2 minutes per side on the grill.
5. Combine all the ingredients for the salad in a large salad bowl and toss.
6. Once the carrots are grilled, slice and add them on top of the salad.
7. Serve fresh.

Nutritional Facts: Calories 91.3; Total Fat 1.8 g; Carbs 16.33 g; Net Carbs 7 g; Fiber 4.6 g; Protein 3.55 g

SNACKS

Mango and Papaya After-Chop

Preparation: 25 minutes	Cooking: 0 minutes	Servings: 1

INGREDIENTS

- ¼ papaya, chopped
- 1 mango, chopped
- 1 tbsp coconut milk
- ½ tsp agave syrup

DIRECTIONS

1. Cut open the papaya. Scoop out the seeds chop.
2. Peel the mango. Slice the fruit from the pit chop.
3. Put the fruit in a bowl. Add the remaining ingredients. Stir to coat.

Nutritional Facts: Calories 100; Fats 1 g; Carbohydrates 25 g; Proteins 1 g

Raspberry Chia Pudding Shots

Preparation: 1 hour	Cooking: 15 minutes	Servings: 2

INGREDIENTS

- ¼ cup chia seeds
- ½ cup raspberries
- ½ cup coconut milk
- ¼ cup almond milk
- 1 tbsp cacao powder
-

DIRECTIONS

1. Combine all the ingredients except for the raspberries in a jar.
2. Let sit for 2–3 minutes and transfer to shot glasses.
3. Refrigerate for 1 hour or overnight to serve as breakfast.
4. Serve with fresh raspberries.

Nutritional Facts: Calories 240; Fats 19 g; Carbohydrates 5 g; Proteins 5 g

Oatmeal Cookies

Preparation: 10 minutes	Cooking: 15 minutes	Servings: 4

INGREDIENTS

- ¼ cup applesauce
- ½ tsp cinnamon
- 1/3 cup raisins
- ½ tsp vanilla extract, pure
- 1 cup ripe banana, mashed
- 2 cups oatmeal

DIRECTIONS

1. Preheat your oven to 350°F.
2. Take a bowl and mix in everything until you have a gooey mixture
3. Pour the batter into an ungreased baking sheet drop by drop and flatten them using a tbsp
4. Transfer to your oven; bake for 15 minutes
5. Serve once ready!

Nutritional Facts: Calories 80; Fat 1 g; Carbohydrates 16 g; Protein 2 g

Almond Butter Brownies

Preparation: 30 minutes   **Cooking: 20 minutes**   **Servings: 4**

INGREDIENTS

- 1 scoop protein powder
- 2 tbsp cocoa powder
- ½ cup almond butter, melted
- 1 cup bananas, overripe

DIRECTIONS

1. Preheat the oven to 350°F/ 176°C.
2. Spray the brownie tray with cooking spray.
3. Add all the ingredients into the blender and blend until smooth.
4. Pour the batter into the prepared dish and bake in a preheated oven for 20 minutes.
5. Serve and enjoy.

Nutritional Facts: Calories 82; Fat 2.1 g; Carbohydrates 11.4 g; Protein 6.9 g; Cholesterol 16 mg.

Roasted Almonds

Preparation: 5 minutes   **Cooking: 6 minutes**   **Servings: 8**

INGREDIENTS

- 2 cups almonds
- 1 tbsp garlic powder
- ¼ tsp ground black pepper
- 1 tsp paprika
- 1 tbsp soy sauce

DIRECTIONS

1. Switch on the air fryer, insert the fryer basket, then shut it with the lid, set the frying temperature at 320°F, and let it preheat for 5 minutes.
2. Meanwhile, take a large bowl, add almonds to it, then add the remaining ingredients and toss until mixed.
3. Open the preheated fryer, place almonds in it, close the lid, and cook for 6 minutes until golden brown and cooked, shaking halfway.
4. When done, the air fryer will beep, then open the lid and transfer almonds to a dish.
5. Serve straight away.

Nutritional Facts: Calories 7.7; Fat 0.7 g; Carbs 0.3 g; Protein 0.3 g; Fiber 0.1 g

Tomato and Pesto Toast

Preparation: 5 minutes   **Cooking: 0 minute**   **Servings: 4**

INGREDIENTS

- 1 small tomato, sliced
- ¼ tsp ground black pepper
- 1 tbsp vegan pesto
- 2 tbsp hummus
- 1 slice of wholewheat bread, toasted
- Hemp seeds, as needed for garnishing

DIRECTIONS

1. Spread the hummus on one side of the toast, top with tomato slices, and then drizzle with pesto.
2. Sprinkle black pepper on the toast along with hemp seeds, and then serve straight away.

Nutritional Facts: Calories 214; Fat 7.2 g; Carbs 32 g; Protein 6.5 g; Fiber 3 g

Avocado and Sprout Toast

Preparation: 5 minutes	Cooking: 0 minute	Servings: 4

INGREDIENTS

- ½ a medium avocado, sliced
- 1 slice wholewheat bread, toasted
- 2 tbsp sprouts
- 2 tbsp hummus
- ¼ tsp lemon zest
- ½ tsp hemp seeds
- ¼ tsp red pepper flakes

DIRECTIONS

1. Spread the hummus on one side of the toast and then top with avocado slices and sprouts.
2. Sprinkle with lemon zest, hemp seeds and red pepper flakes, and then serve straight away.

Nutritional Facts: Calories 200; Fat 10.5 g; Carbs 22 g; Protein 7 g; Fiber 7 g

Apple and Hummus Toast

Preparation: 5 minutes	Cooking: 0 minute	Servings: 4

INGREDIENTS

- ½ a small apple, cored, sliced
- 1 slice wholewheat bread, toasted
- 1 tbsp agave syrup
- 2 tbsp hummus
- 1/8 tsp cinnamon

DIRECTIONS

1. Spread the hummus on one side of the toast, top with apple slices, and then drizzle with agave syrup.
2. Sprinkle cinnamon on it and then serve straight away.

Nutritional Facts: Calories 212; Fat 7 g; Carbs 35 g; Protein 4 g; Fiber 5.5 g

Taco Pita Pizzas

Preparation: 5 Minutes	Cooking: 7 Minutes	Servings: 4

INGREDIENTS

- 4 sandwich-size pita bread pieces or Sandwich Thins
- 1 cup vegetarian refried beans
- 1 cup pizza sauce
- 1 cup chopped mushrooms
- 1 tsp minced jalapeño (optional)

DIRECTIONS

1. Preheat the oven to 400°F.
2. Assemble for pizzas: On each pita, spread about ¼ cup of refried beans. Pour ¼ cup of pizza sauce over the beans and spread evenly. Add ¼ cup of mushrooms. Sprinkle ¼ tsp of minced jalapeño (if using) over the mushrooms.
3. Place the pizzas on the ready baking sheet and bake for 7 minutes.
4. Cool completely before placing each pizza in a freezer-safe plastic bag or store together in one large airtight, freezer-safe container with parchment paper between the pizzas.

Nutritional Facts: Calories 148; Fat 2 g; Protein 6 g; Carbohydrates 29 g; Fiber 5 g; Sodium 492 mg

Savory Seed Cracker Bites

Preparation: 10 Minutes   **Cooking: 50 Minutes**   **Servings: 16**

INGREDIENTS

- ½ cup sunflower seeds
- ½ cup pumpkin seeds
- 1/3 cup chia seeds
- ½ cup sesame seeds
- ¾ tsp minced garlic
- 1 tsp soy sauce or tamari
- 1 tsp vegan Worcestershire sauce
- ½ tsp dried oregano
- ½ tsp ground cayenne pepper
- ½ cup water

DIRECTIONS

1. Set oven to 325°F and preheat. Take a rimmed baking sheet and line it with parchment paper.
2. Combine the sunflower seeds, pumpkin seeds, chia seeds, sesame seeds, garlic, soy sauce, Worcestershire sauce, oregano, cayenne, and water in a bowl. Pour this mixture on the prepared baking sheet, making sure to spread it evenly to cover the entire sheet to the rim.
3. Bake the mixture for 25 minutes. Then, take the pan out of the oven and flip the mixture over on the other side, in order to cook the wet. Bake for an extra 20 to 25 minutes or until the sides are browned.
4. Let it cool completely before breaking it up into about 16 pieces. Divide the crackers among 4 glass jars with lids.

Nutritional Facts: For 4 crackers Calories 260; Fat 22g; Protein 10 g; Carbohydrates 12 g; Fiber 6 g; Sodium 76 mg

Spinach Chips

Preparation: 10 minutes   **Cooking: 20 minutes**   **Servings: 4**

INGREDIENTS

- 1 pound baby spinach, well dried
- black pepper, to the taste
- ½ tsp oregano, dried
- 1 tsp sweet paprika
- cooking spray

DIRECTIONS

1. Oiled a baking sheet using cooking spray and spread the spinach leaves on it. Add the other ingredients, toss gently, and bake at 435°F for 20 minutes. Serve as a snack.

Nutritional Facts: Calories 140; Fat 4.2 g; Carbs 6 g; Protein 4 g

Balsamic Zucchini Bowls

Preparation: 10 minutes   **Cooking: 3 hours**   **Servings: 8**

INGREDIENTS

- 3 zucchinis, thinly sliced
- Black pepper, to the taste
- 2 tbsp avocado oil
- 1 tsp turmeric powder
- 1 tsp coriander, ground
- 2 tbsp balsamic vinegar

DIRECTIONS

1. Spread the zucchini on a lined baking sheet and mix it with the other ingredients. Toss and bake at 360°F for 3 hours. Divide into bowls and serve as a snack.

Nutritional Facts: Calories 47.6; Fat 3.68 g; Carbs 3.3 g; Protein 0.9 g

Peanut Butter–Mocha Energy Bites

Preparation: 45 minutes	Cooking: 0 minutes	Servings: 12

INGREDIENTS

- ¼ cup creamy peanut butter
- 2 tbsp agave syrup
- 1 tbsp non-dairy milk or water, plus more as needed
- 1 to 2 tsp instant coffee powder or chopped roasted coffee beans (optional)
- 2 tbsp date paste
- 2 tbsp unsweetened cocoa powder
- 1 tbsp ground flaxseed
- ½ cup cooked quinoa
- 2 tbsp plant-based protein powder, coconut flour, or ground almonds

DIRECTIONS

1. Stir the peanut butter, agave syrup and milk in a large bowl until smooth. Add the coffee powder (if using), date paste, cocoa powder and flaxseed; stir to combine.
2. Stir in the quinoa and protein powder. Drizzle in another tbsp of milk to moisten, if needed.
3. Divide the mixture into about 12 portions, and roll each into a small ball. Place them on a plate and chill, if you can, for 30 minutes.
4. You can keep it in an airtight container in the refrigerator for up to 1 week. If you don't have a fridge, enjoy them the same day.

Nutritional Facts: Calories 70; Protein 3 g; Fat 3 g; Carbohydrates 8 g

Cinnamon Chickpea Energy Bites

Preparation: 35 minutesCooking: 0 minutesServings: **16**

INGREDIENTS

- ¾ cup canned chickpeas drained and rinsed
- 1/3 cup unsweetened shredded coconut
- ¼ cup date paste
- 1 tsp ground cinnamon or pumpkin pie spice
- 2 tbsp vegan dark chocolate chips

DIRECTIONS

1. In a food processor, combine the chickpeas, coconut, date paste and cinnamon. Purée until smooth, occasionally pausing to scrape down the sides of the bowl as needed. Taste for sweetness.
2. If it still tastes "beany," add more date paste, 2 tbsp at a time, until you like the taste. Pulse to combine.
3. Put the chocolate chips, then pulse a few times to chop them and combine them in the mixture. Divide the batter into 16 portions and form each into a small ball.
4. Place them on a plate and refrigerate, if you can, for 20 minutes. Serve.

Nutritional Facts: Calories 62; Protein 1 g; Fat 4 g; Carbohydrates 7 g

5-Ingredient Granola Bars

Preparation: 35 minutes   **Cooking: 0 minutes**   **Servings: 12**

INGREDIENTS

- ½ cup peanut butter, almond/cashew butter/sunflower seed butter
- ¼ cup agave syrup
- ¼ cup ground almonds or plant-based protein powder
- 1½ cup rolled oats
- ¼ cup dried cranberries

DIRECTIONS

1. Stir the peanut butter and agave syrup in a large bowl until smooth. Put the protein powder, oats, plus cranberries, and mix.
2. Press granola into an 8-inch baking dish, then refrigerate within 15 minutes. Cut into 12 bars.
3. You can keep them in an airtight container in the refrigerator for up to 1 week or at room temperature for about 4 days.

Nutritional Facts: Calories 151; Protein 7 g; Fat 6 g; Carbohydrates 19 g

Banana–Chocolate Chip Muffins

Preparation: 15 minutes   **Cooking: 20–25 minutes**   **Servings: 12**

INGREDIENTS

- 2 tbsp coconut oil or vegan margarine, melted, plus more for coating the muffin tin (optional)
- 3 bananas
- ½ cup non-dairy milk or plain non-dairy yogurt
- ½ cup date paste
- 2 tbsp ground flaxseed
- 1 tsp vanilla extract
- 1 tsp apple cider vinegar
- 1 cup rice flour
- 1 cup wholewheat flour
- 1 tsp baking powder
- ½ tsp baking soda
- ½ cup vegan dark chocolate chips

DIRECTIONS

1. Preheat the oven to 400°F. Coat a muffin tin with coconut oil, line it with paper muffin cups, or use a nonstick tin.
2. In a large bowl, use a fork to mash the bananas. Stir in the milk, date paste, flaxseed, coconut oil, vanilla and vinegar.
3. Add the rice flour and wholewheat flour, baking powder and baking soda; stir until just combined. Fold in the chocolate chips without stirring too much.
4. Scoop the mixture into the prepared tin, about 1/3 cup for each muffin. Bake for 20 to 25 minutes until the top is slightly browned and springy to the touch.
5. Let it cool for about 10 minutes. Slide a dinner knife around the inside of each cup to loosen the muffins, then tilt them on their sides in the muffin wells to allow air to get underneath. Serve.

Nutritional Facts: Calories 143.27; Protein 3 g; Fat 0.9 g; Carbohydrates 31.7 g

BREAD, CRACKERS, ENERGY BARS, BISCUITS

Forest Mushroom Loaf

Preparation + Cook Time: 20 minutes Servings: **2**

INGREDIENTS

- 2 cups mushrooms, chopped
- ½ cups vegan cheese, shredded
- ¾ cup flour
- 2 tbsp vegan butter, melted
- ½ Silken Tofu

DIRECTIONS

1. In a food processor, pulse together the mushrooms, cheese, flour, melted butter and tofu until a uniform consistency is achieved.
2. Transfer into a silicone loaf pan, spreading and leveling with a palette knife.
3. Preheat the fryer to 375°F and put the rack inside.
4. Set the loaf pan on the rack and cook for 15 minutes.
5. Take care when removing the pan from the fryer and leave it to cool. Then slice and serve.

Nutritional Facts: Calories 390.8; Fat 17.48 g; Carbs 46.17 g; Protein 12.7 g

Delicious Vegan Cheese Bread

Preparation: 10 Minutes	Cooking: 35 Minutes	Servings: 12

INGREDIENTS

- ½ cup silken tofu
- 2 cups wholewheat flour
- ½ cup vegan butter, melted
- 1 cup unsweetened non-dairy milk
- ½ tsp baking soda
- ½ tsp baking powder
- 1 tsp brown rice syrup
- 1 cup vegan cheddar cheese, shredded
- pepper
- ½ tsp cilantro

DIRECTIONS

1. Preheat the oven to 350°F. In a large mixing bowl, mix flour, baking soda, baking powder, brown rice syrup, cheese, pepper and cilantro.
2. In a small bowl, mix tofu with no-dairy milk and vegan butter. Add the tofu mixture to the flour mixture and mix well.
3. Transfer the mixture into the greased 9.5-inch loaf pan and bake in a preheated oven for 35–40 minutes.
4. Allow cooling for 15 minutes. Slice and serve.

Nutritional Facts: Calories 180.9; Carbs 17.9 g; Fat 9.7 g; Protein 5.23 g

Strawberry Bread

Preparation: 15 Minutes   **Cooking: 60 Minutes**   **Servings: 10**

INGREDIENTS

- ½ cup silken tofu
- 2 cups wholewheat flour
- 1 tsp vanilla
- ½ cup vegetable stock
- 1 tsp baking soda
- ½ tsp cinnamon
- 2 cups brown rice syrup
- 2¼ cups fresh strawberries, chopped
- ½ tsp saffron

DIRECTIONS

1. Preheat the oven to 350°F. Grease a 9.5-inch loaf pan and set it aside.
2. In a mixing bowl, mix together flour, baking soda, cinnamon, brown rice syrup and saffron.
3. In a separate bowl, tofu, vanilla and vegetable stock. Stir in strawberries.
4. Add the flour mixture to the tofu mixture and stir until well combined.
5. Pour the batter into the prepared loaf pan and bake in a preheated oven for 50–60 minutes.
6. Allow cooling for 10–15 minutes. Slice and serve.

Nutritional Facts: Calories 316; Carbs 73.5 g; Fat 0.5 g; Protein 4.7 g

Moist Banana Bread

Preparation: 10 Minutes   **Cooking: 60 Minutes**   **Servings: 6**

INGREDIENTS

- ½ cup silken tofu
- 1 tsp baking powder
- ½ cup Brown rice syrup
- 1 tsp vanilla
- ½ cup vegan butter, melted
- 3 ripe bananas
- 1 ½ cup wholewheat flour
- pinch saffron

DIRECTIONS

1. Preheat the oven to 350°F. In a large bowl, add bananas and mash until smooth. Add silken tofu, vanilla and butter, and mix well.
2. Add flour, baking powder, brown rice syrup and saffron, and mix until well combined.
3. Pour the batter into the greased loaf pan and bake in a preheated oven for 60 minutes. Slice and serve.

Nutritional Facts: Calories 391.4; Carbs 59.22 g; Fat 15.5 g; Protein 5.17 g

DESSERTS

Chocolate Mousse

Preparation: 5 minutes	Cooking: 0 minute	Servings: 2

INGREDIENTS

- 1/2 tbsp agave syrup
- ½ tsp cinnamon
- 3 tbsp cocoa powder, unsweetened
- 1 cup coconut milk

DIRECTIONS

1. On the day before, place the coconut milk into the refrigerator overnight.
2. Remove the coconut milk from the refrigerator; it should be very thick.
3. Whisk in cocoa powder with an electric mixer.
4. Add syrup and cinnamon, and whip until combined.
5. Place in individual bowls, serve and enjoy.

Nutritional Facts: Calories 130; Fat 5 g; Fiber 3 g; Carbs 6 g; Protein 7 g

Chocolate Macaroons

Preparation: 15 minutes	Cooking: 15 minutes	Servings: 8

INGREDIENTS

- 1 cup unsweetened shredded coconut
- 2/3 cup coconut milk
- 2 tbsp cocoa powder
- ¼ cup agave

DIRECTIONS

1. Preheat the oven to 350°F. Line a baking sheet with parchment paper. In a medium saucepan, cook all the fixings over medium-high heat until you have a firm dough. Scoop the dough into balls and place them on the baking sheet.
2. Bake for 15 minutes, remove from the oven and let them cool on the baking sheet. Serve cooled macaroons.

Nutritional Facts: Calories 141; Carbs 1 g; Fat 8 g; Protein 1 g

Chocolate Pudding

Preparation: 5 minutes	Cooking: 0 minutes	Servings: 1

INGREDIENTS

- 1 banana
- 2 to 4 tbsp non-dairy milk
- 2 tbsp unsweetened cocoa powder
- 2 tbsp date paste (optional)
- ½ ripe avocado or 1 cup silken tofu (optional)

DIRECTIONS

1. In a small blender, combine the banana, milk, cocoa powder, date paste (if using) and avocado (if using). Purée until smooth. Alternatively, in a small bowl, mash the banana very well and stir in the remaining ingredients.

Nutritional Facts: Calories 244; Protein 4 g; Fat 3 g; Carbohydrates 59 g

Lime and Watermelon Granita

Preparation: 6 hours and 15 minutes   **Cooking: 0 minutes**   **Servings: 4**

INGREDIENTS

- 8 cups seedless watermelon chunks
- juice 2 limes or 2 tbsp prepared lime juice
- ½ cup date paste
- strips lime zest, for garnish

DIRECTIONS

1. Mix the watermelon, lime juice, plus date paste in a blender or food processor, and process until smooth. After processing, stir well to combine both batches.
2. Pour the mixture into a 9-by-13-inch glass dish. Freeze for 2 to 3 hours. Remove, then use a fork to scrape the top layer of ice. Leave the shaved ice on top and return it to the freezer.
3. In another hour, remove from the freezer and repeat. Do this a few more times until all the ice is scraped up. Serve frozen, garnished with strips of lime zest.

Nutritional Facts: Calories 70; Carbs 18 g; Fat 0 g; Protein 1 g

Orange and Cranberry Quinoa Bites

Preparation: 10 minutes   **Cooking: 0 minutes**   **Servings: 12 bites**

INGREDIENTS

- 3 tbsp almond butter, or alternative seed butter
- 2 tbsp maple syrup
- 1 cup cooked quinoa
- 1/3 cup toasted sesame seeds
- 1 tbsp chia seeds
- ½ tsp almond extract, or vanilla extract
- zest 1 orange
- 2 tbsp dried cranberries
- 1/3 cup ground almonds

DIRECTIONS

1. Mix in a medium bowl the syrup and nut or seed butter until you have a smooth consistency. Next, mix in the rest of the ingredients and stir them to make sure it holds together to form a ball. Shape the mixture into 14 separate balls.
2. Put them onto a baking sheet covered with parchment paper and put them in the fridge to set for at least 15 minutes.
3. If the quinoa balls aren't keeping their shape, it's probably due to the amount of moisture in the cooked quinoa. Add some more nut or seed butter mixed with some syrup to increase the stickiness.

Nutrition Facts: (1 bite) Calories: 120; Total Fat: 11 g; Carbs: 14 g; Fiber: 4.5 g; Protein: 4 g

Cocoa Cashew Truffles

Preparation: 15 minutes   **Cooking: 0 minutes**   **Servings: 14**

INGREDIENTS

- 1 cup raw cashews, soaked in water overnight
- 1 cup pitted dates
- 1 cup unsweetened shredded coconut
- 2 tbsp avocado oil
- 1 ½ tbsp cocoa powder

DIRECTIONS

1. Take your food processor and combine the cashews, dates, ½ cup of shredded coconut, avocado oil, and cocoa powder.
2. Pulse the mixture until everything is fully mixed together; it should look like a chunky cookie dough substance. Spread the remaining ½ cup of your shredded coconut onto a plate.
3. Form tbsp-size balls and roll on the shredded coconut pieces on a plate. Then transfer to a parchment paper-lined plate or baking sheet. Repeat this process for all 14 truffles.
4. Put the truffles in your refrigerator for at least an 1 hour to set. Then, transfer the truffles into some form of a storage container.

Nutritional Facts: Calories 252; Fat 20 g; Protein 3.2 g; Carbohydrates 17 g

Almond date and apricot energy bites

Preparation: 5 minutes   **Servings: 24 bites**

INGREDIENTS

- 1 cup dates, pitted
- 1 cup of chopped dry apricots
- 1 cup unsweetened shredded coconut
- ¾ cup ground almonds
- ¼ cup chia seeds
- ¼ cup cocoa nibs, or non-dairy chocolate chips

DIRECTIONS

1. Purée all the ingredients in a food processor until crumbly and sticking together, making sure to push down the sides to keep it blending. In alternative to a food processor, you can mash soft Medjool dates. Use the softest dates you can find. Medjool dates are the best for this purpose. But with harder baking dates that take a long time to blend up, you'll have to soak them in water for at least an hour to be able to purée them in a blender.
2. Form the mix into 24 balls and place them on a baking sheet lined with parchment or waxed paper and place in the fridge to harden for at least 15 minutes.

Nutrition Facts: (1 bite) Calories: 152; Total Fat: 11 g; Carbs: 13 g; Fiber: 5 g; Protein: 3 g

Exotic Cream Pie

Preparation: 50 minutes   **Cooking: 0 minutes**   **Servings: 8**

INGREDIENTS

FOR THE CRUST:

- ¾ cup rolled oats
- 1 cup cashews

FOR THE FILLING:

- 1 cup unsweetened coconut milk
- ½ cup water
- 2 mangos, peeled and chopped (should be about 2 cups)
- ¼ cup passion fruit pulp
- ¾ cup shredded coconut
- 1 ¼ cup pitted dates

DIRECTIONS

1. Place all the crust fixings in a food processor and pulse until it sticks together. Press the mixture into an 8-inch pie pan.
2. In a blender purée all the ingredients for the filling until smooth (this should take about 1 minute). It should be quite thick.
3. Put the filling into the crust and smooth the top. Next put the pie in the freezer until set for at least 30 minutes. You need to take it out for about 15 minutes once it has frozen so that it can soften before serving.
4. Add some coconut whipped cream on top once the pie has set. Then sprinkle toasted shredded coconut.

Nutritional Facts: Calories 430; Fat 27 g; Carbs 46 g; Protein 9 g

Cherry-Vanilla Rice Pudding

Preparation: 15 minutes   **Cooking: 30 minutes**   **Servings: 4–6**

INGREDIENTS

- 1 cup short-grain brown rice
- 1¾ cups unsweet. non-dairy milk, plus more as needed
- 1 ½ cup water
- 4 tbsp pure agave syrup, plus more as needed
- 1 tsp vanilla extract (use ½ tsp if you use vanilla milk)
- ¼ cup dried cherries or ½ cup fresh or frozen pitted cherries

DIRECTIONS

1. In your electric pressure cooker's cooking pot, combine the rice, milk, water, syrup and vanilla. Select High Pressure for 30 minutes.
2. Let the pressure release naturally, within 20 minutes. Unlock and remove the lid.
3. Add the cherries while stirring and put the lid back on loosely for about 10 minutes. Serve, adding more milk as desired.

Nutritional Facts: Calories 177; Fat 1 g; Protein 3 g; Carbs 2 g

Chia Raspberry Pudding

Preparation: 10 minutes   **Chilling: 3 Hours**   **Servings: 2**

INGREDIENTS

- 4 tbsp chia seeds
- ½ cup raspberries
- 1 cup coconut milk

DIRECTIONS

1. Add the raspberry and coconut milk into your blender, and blend until smooth.
2. Pour the mixture into a mason jar.
3. Add chia seeds and stir.
4. Cap the jar and shake.
5. Set in the fridge for 3 hours.
6. Serve and enjoy!

Nutrition Facts: Calories: 408 Fat: 38.8 g Net Carbs: 22.3 g Protein: 9.1 g

ICE CREAMS AND SMOOTHIES

Strawberry Ice Cream

| Preparation: 5 minutes | Cooking: 0 minutes | Servings: 3 |

INGREDIENTS

- ½ cup stevia
- 1 tbsp lemon juice
- ¾ cup non-dairy coffee creamer
- 10 oz. strawberries
- 1 cup crushed ice

DIRECTIONS

1. Blend everything in a blender until smooth.
2. Freeze until frozen.
3. Serve.

Nutritional Facts: Calories 94.4; Fat 6 g; Carb 8.3 g; Phosphorus 25 mg; Potassium 108 mg; Sodium 25 mg; Protein 1.3 g

Mango Passion fruit Ice cream

| Preparation: 45 Minutes | Cooking: 0 Minutes | Servings: 2 |

INGREDIENTS

- 2 fresh ripe mangoes
- 1.5 cups frozen mango chunks
- 1 can coconut milk (thick part from the top of can only)
- 3 passion fruit
- 2 tsp vanilla extract
- juice ½ a lime

DIRECTIONS

1. Blend all the ingredients until smooth.
2. Put the mixture in an ice cream maker for 40 minutes.
3. Add more passion fruit on top and serve.

Nutritional Facts: Calories 303.77; Carbs 32.44; Fat 19.95; Fiber 4.4 g; Protein 3.5 g

Vegan Chocolate Ice Cream

| Preparation: 10 Minutes | Freezing: 25 Minutes | Servings: 6 |

INGREDIENTS

- 1 ½ cup cashews raw, unsalted if available
- 1 cup dates, pitted and packed 22 deglet noor dates
- 3 cups water including ice
- ¼–1/3 cup cocoa powder more for a richer, dark chocolate flavor
- 1 tsp vanilla

DIRECTIONS

1. Combine cashews and dates in 3 cups of water for roughly 2 minutes, or until smooth, taking caution not to blend for too long and warm the mixture.
2. Blend in the vanilla until completely smooth.
3. If feasible, refrigerate for another hour or more.

Nutritional Facts: Calories 275; Carbs 32; Fat 16.39; Fiber 3.7 g; Protein 6.3 g

Chocolate Banana Ice Cream

Preparation: 5 minutes   **Freezing: 45 Minutes**   **Servings: 1 to 2**

INGREDIENTS

- 1 tbsp agave optional
- 3 frozen bananas
- 3 tbsp peanut butter
- 1 tbsp cocoa powder
-
- ½ tsp vanilla extract optional NOTES:

DIRECTIONS

1. Pulse all ingredients in a food processor or high-powered blender, except for bananas. When well blended, pulse or puree the frozen sliced bananas until the ice cream is thick and creamy.
2. Scoop into a dish or ice cream cones and serve right away.

NOTE:

3. *You don't need to use milk if you have a Vitamix. If you're using something else, add a spoonful of* milk at a time until it's smooth.
4. If you want it to firm up even more, place it in a loaf pan or storage container and place it in the freezer for 45 minutes to an hour.

Nutritional Facts: Calories 280; Carbs 70 g; Protein 3 g; Fat 1 g; Fiber 7 g

Chocolate Peanut Butter Crispy Bars

Preparation: 45 minutes   **Cooking: 0 minutes**   **Servings: 6–8**

INGREDIENTS

- 1 cup dates
- 1 cup raw cashews
- ¼ cup Dutch-process cocoa powder
- 1 tsp vanilla extract
- 1(½) cup crunchy vegan peanut butter
- 2 cups dairy-free chocolate chips
- 1 cup all-natural smooth vegan peanut butter
- 3 cups puffed rice cereal

DIRECTIONS

1. Prepare an 8-inch square baking dish lined using parchment paper. Set aside. Soak the dates in a bowl of warm water for 10 minutes. Drain and pat dry.
2. In a food processor or blender, combine the dates, cashews, cocoa powder and vanilla extract, and process to form a thick dough.
3. Press into the baking dish. Cover with the crunchy peanut butter, spreading it into an even layer. Refrigerate for 5 minutes.
4. In a large microwave-safe bowl, combine the chocolate chips and smooth peanut butter. Microwave in 30-second increments, stirring in between, until smooth. Remove from the microwave and stir in the puffed rice cereal, mixing to coat.
5. Pour the puffed rice mixture over the chunky peanut butter layer in the baking dish and press flat. Refrigerate for at least 30 minutes. Remove, then cut into squares.

Nutritional Facts: Calories 977; Fat 66 g; Carbs 83 g; Protein 26 g

Beet and Berry Smoothie

Preparation: 5 Minutes	Cooking: 0 Minutes	Servings: 2

INGREDIENTS

- 1 cup water, chilled
- 2 tbsp lemon juice
- 4 tsp vegetable stock
- 2 tbsp agave syrup
- 4 cups mixed frozen strawberries and raspberries
- 2 small red beets, peeled, sliced

DIRECTIONS

1. Plug in a high-powered blender, and then add all the ingredients into it in the order mentioned in the ingredients list.
2. Pulse for 45 to 60 seconds or more depending on the blender until well combined and smooth, and then distribute the smoothie between 2 glasses.
3. Serve straight away.

Nutritional Facts: Calories 300; Total Fat 11 g; Saturated Fat 8 g; Carbohydrates 60 g; Fiber 10 g; Protein 4 g.

Orange Resolution Smoothie

Preparation: 5 Minutes	Cooking: 0 Minutes	Servings: 2

INGREDIENTS

- ½ cup orange juice
- 1 cup Greek yogurt (plant-based)
- 1 cup frozen mango chunks
- 2 bananas, peeled, frozen
- ½ cup miniature carrots
- 1 cup frozen peach slices
- 2 tbsp agave syrup
- ½ cup pineapple pieces

DIRECTIONS

1. Gather all the ingredients.
2. Plug in a high-powered blender, and then add all the ingredients into it in the order mentioned in the ingredients list.
3. Pulse for 45 to 60 seconds or more depending on the blender until well combined and smooth, and then distribute the smoothie between two glasses.
4. Serve straight away.

Nutritional Facts: Calories 199; Total Fat 6 g; Saturated Fat 4.5 g; Carbohydrates 34 g; Fiber 3 g; Protein 5 g

Mango and Cucumber Smoothie

Preparation: 5 Minutes	Cooking: 0 Minutes	Servings: 2

INGREDIENTS

- 1 ½ cup coconut milk, unsweetened
- 4 tsp lime juice
- 1 cup baby spinach leaves, fresh, rinsed
- 2 cup mango pieces, fresh or frozen
- 4 mint leaves, rinsed
- 1 cup chopped cucumber, deseeded, peeled
- ¼ tsp cayenne pepper
- 1 cup ice cubes

DIRECTIONS

4. Gather all the ingredients.
5. Plug in a high-powered blender, and then add all the ingredients into it in the order mentioned in the ingredients list.
6. Pulse for 45 to 60 seconds or more depending on the blender until well combined and smooth, and then distribute the smoothie between 2 glasses.
7. Serve straight away.

Nutritional Facts: Calories 170; Total Fat 4.6 g; Saturated Fat 0.5 g; Carbohydrates 33.5 g; Fiber 6 g; Protein 2.6 g

Melon, Kale, and Broccoli Smoothie

Preparation: 5 Minutes   Cooking: 0 Minutes   Servings: 2

INGREDIENTS

- 2 cups coconut water, unsweetened
- 2/3 cup broccoli florets
- 2 cups honeydew melon pieces
- 1 lime, peeled, deseeded, halved
- ½ cup kale, destemmed, rinsed
- 2 Medjool dates pitted
- ½ cup mint leaves
- 1 cup ice cubes

DIRECTIONS

1. Gather all the ingredients.
2. Plug in a high-powered blender, and then add all the ingredients into it in the order mentioned in the ingredients list.
3. Pulse for 45 to 60 seconds or more depending on the blender until well combined and smooth, and then distribute the smoothie between 2 glasses.
4. Serve straight away.

Nutritional Facts: Calories 220; Total Fat 1 g; Saturated Fat 0.6 g; Carbohydrates 46 g; Fiber 8.6 g; Protein 5.4 g

Cucumber, Celery, and Apple Smoothie

Preparation: 5 Minutes   Cooking: 0 Minutes   Servings: 2

INGREDIENTS

- 1 cup water, chilled
- ½ lemon, juiced
- 1 large stalk celery
- 2 medium green apples, cored
- 1 large cucumber

DIRECTIONS

1. Gather all the ingredients.
2. Plug in a high-powered blender, and then add all the ingredients into it in the order mentioned in the ingredients list.
3. Pulse for 45 to 60 seconds or more depending on the blender until well combined and smooth, and then distribute the smoothie between 2 glasses.
4. Serve straight away.

Nutritional Facts: Calories 131; Total Fat 0.6 g; Saturated Fat 0.2 g; Carbohydrates 28.8 g; Fiber 6.7 g; Protein 1.3 g

Spicy Carrot, Avocado, and Tomato Smoothie

Preparation: 5 Minutes	Cooking: 0 Minutes	Servings: 2

INGREDIENTS

- 3/4 cup coconut water, unsweetened
- ½ a medium cucumber, unpeeled, chopped
- 1 medium tomato, deseeded, chopped
- 1 avocado, peeled, pitted
- 1 cup chopped romaine lettuce
- 1 medium carrot, peeled, diced
- 1 lime, peeled, halved
- 1 clove garlic, peeled
- 3/4 tsp cilantro
- 1/8 tsp cayenne pepper
- 1 tbsp vegetable stock
- 1 cup ice cubes

DIRECTIONS

1. Gather all the ingredients.
2. Plug in a high-powered blender, and then add all the ingredients into it in the order mentioned in the ingredients list.
3. Pulse for 45 to 60 seconds or more depending on the blender until well combined and smooth, and then distribute the smoothie between 2 glasses.
4. Serve straight away.

Nutritional Facts: Calories 244; Total Fat 17 g; Saturated Fat 2.6 g; Carbohydrates 19.2 g; Fiber 9.2 g; Protein 3 g

Kale and Peanut Butter Smoothie

Preparation: 5 minutes	Cooking: 0 minutes	Servings: 4

INGREDIENTS

- 4 frozen bananas, sliced
- 2 cups kale
- ½ cup peanut butter
- 2/3 cups coconut milk, unsweetened

DIRECTIONS

1. Place all ingredients in a food processor or blender, then blend for 1-2 minutes until well blended, scraping the sides of the container frequently.
2. Distribute the smoothie among glasses and then serve.

Nutritional Facts: Calories 390; Fat 19 g; Carbohydrates 42 g; Fiber 7 g; Protein 15 g;

SAUCES AND TOPPINGS

Light Vegetable Broth

Preparation: 30 minutes   **Cooking: 3 to 4 hours**   **Servings: about 8 quarts**

INGREDIENTS

- 6 ½ quarts water
- 2 cups white wine or unsweetened apple juice
- 6 carrots, scrubbed and coarsely chopped
- 6 stalks celery, thickly sliced
- 2 large onions, chopped
- 2 large potatoes, scrubbed and coarsely chopped
- 3 medium zucchinis, thickly sliced
- ½ pound mushrooms, cleaned and left whole
- 1 leek, white part only, cleaned and thickly sliced
- 5 to 6 cloves garlic, crushed
- 2 bay leaves
- Several large sprigs fresh thyme
- Several large sprigs fresh parsley
- 10 whole peppercorns

DIRECTIONS

1. Combine all the ingredients in a large soup pot or stockpot and bring to a boil.
2. When it starts to boil, reduce the heat to low, cover, and allow it to simmer for 3 to 4 hours, stirring occasionally, or until the vegetables are very soft.
3. Strain the broth through a fine-mesh strainer and discard the vegetables.
4. Let the broth cool to room temperature and refrigerate until ready to use.

Nutritional Facts: Calories 194; Fat 0.5 g; Carbs 42.8 g; Protein 4.6 g; Fiber 6.1 g

Pinto Bean Dip

Preparation: 5 minutes   **Cooking: 0 minutes**   **Servings: 1 ½ cup**

INGREDIENTS

- 15 oz. canned pinto beans
- 1 jalapeno pepper
- 2 tsp ground cumin
- 3 tbsp nutritional yeast
- 1/3 cup basil salsa

DIRECTIONS

1. Place all the ingredients in a food processor, cover with the lid, and then pulse until smooth.
2. Tip the dip in a bowl, and then serve with vegetable slices.

Nutritional Facts: Calories 360; Fat 0 g; Protein 24 g; Carbs 72 g; Fiber 24 g

Tamari Vinegar Sauce

Preparation: 10 minutes   **Cooking: 0 minutes**   **Servings: 1 ¼ cups**

INGREDIENTS

- ¼ cup tamari
- ½ cup nutritional yeast
- 2 tbsp balsamic vinegar
- 2 tbsp apple cider vinegar
- 2 tbsp vegan Worcestershire sauce
- 2 tsp vegan Dijon mustard
- 1 tbsp plus 1 tsp maple syrup
- ½ tsp ground turmeric
- ¼ tsp black pepper

DIRECTIONS

1. Place all the ingredients in an airtight container and whisk until everything is well incorporated. Store in the refrigerator for up to 3 weeks.

Nutritional Facts: Calories 216; Fat 9.9 g; Carbs 18.0 g; Protein 13.7 g; Fiber 7.7 g

Chipotle Lime Dressing

Preparation: 5 minutes   **Cooking: 0 minutes**   **Servings: 8**

INGREDIENTS

- ¼ tsp garlic powder
- ¼ tsp paprika
- 1 tbsp agave nectar
- 1 red pepper, chopped
- 3 tbsp lime juice
- 3 tbsp veganize

DIRECTIONS

1. Mix all the ingredients well in a shaker jar or in a blender.

Nutritional Facts: Calories 32; Fat 0.3 g; Fiber 1.5 g; Carbs 0.4 g; Protein 0.4 g

Creamy Spinach and Avocado Dressing

Preparation: 10 minutes   **Cooking: 0 minutes**   **Servings: about 1 cup**

INGREDIENTS

- 2 oz. (57 g) spinach leaves (about 1 cup chopped and packed)
- ¼ medium, ripe avocados
- ¼ cup water, plus more as needed
- 1 small clove garlic
- 1 tbsp vegan Dijon mustard
- 1 green onion, white and green parts, sliced

DIRECTIONS

1. Blitz all the ingredients in a blender until thoroughly mixed. Add a little water if you want a thicker consistency
2. Refrigerate in an airtight container for 3 days and shake before using.

Nutritional Facts: Calories 14.6; Fat 1.0 g; Carbs 1.0 g; Protein 0.4 g; Fiber 0.7 g;

Avocado-Chickpea Dip

Preparation: 15 minutes   **Cooking: 0 minutes**   **Servings: about 2 cups**

INGREDIENTS

- 1 (15-oz. / 425-g) can cooked chickpeas, drained and rinsed
- 2 large, ripe avocados, chopped
- ¼ cup red onion, finely chopped
- 1 tbsp vegan Dijon mustard
- 1 to 2 tbsp lemon juice
- 2 tsp chopped fresh oregano
- ½ tsp garlic clove, finely chopped

DIRECTIONS

1. In a medium bowl, mash the cooked chickpeas. Use a potato masher or simply the back of a fork until the chickpeas pop open (a food processor works best for this).
2. Stir in the remaining ingredients and continue to mash until completely smooth.
3. Place in the refrigerator to chill until ready to serve.

Nutritional Facts: Calories 101; Fat: 1.9 g; Carbs 16.2 g; Protein 4.7 g; Fiber 4.6 g

Beer "Cheese" Dip

Preparation: 10 minutes   **Cooking: 7 minutes**   **Servings: about 3 cups**

INGREDIENTS

- ¾ cup water
- ¾ cup brown ale
- ½ cup raw walnuts, soaked in hot water for at least 15 minutes, then drained
- ½ cup raw cashews, soaked in hot water for at least 15 minutes, then drained
- 2 tbsp tomato paste
- 2 tbsp fresh lemon juice
- 1 tbsp apple cider vinegar
- ½ cup nutritional yeast
- ½ tsp sweet or smoked paprika
- 1 tbsp arrowroot powder
- 1 tbsp red miso

DIRECTIONS

1. Place the water, brown ale, walnuts, cashews, tomato paste, lemon juice and apple cider vinegar into a high-speed blender, and purée until thoroughly mixed and smooth.
2. Transfer the mixture to a saucepan over medium heat. Add the nutritional yeast, paprika and arrowroot powder, and whisk well. Bring to a simmer for about 7 minutes, stirring frequently, or until the mixture begins to thicken and bubble.
3. Remove from the heat and whisk in the red miso. Let the dip cool for 10 minutes and refrigerate in an airtight container for up to 5 days.

Nutritional Facts: Calories 113; Fat: 5.1 g; Carbs 10.4 g; Protein 6.3 g; Fiber 3.8 g

Easy Cucumber Dip

Preparation: 5 minutes   **Cooking: 0 minutes**   **Servings: 1 ½ cup**

INGREDIENTS

- 1 cucumber, peeled, cut in half lengthwise, deseeded, and coarsely chopped
- 3 to 4 cloves garlic, crushed
- 1 cup plain soy yogurt
- ¼ tsp white pepper

DIRECTIONS

1. In a blender, blend the cucumber until finely chopped. Remove from the blender and place in a very fine strainer. Press out as much water as possible. Return to the blender.
2. Add the remaining ingredients and process until smooth.
3. Refrigerate for several hours before serving.

Nutritional Facts: Calories 48; Fat 1.0 g; Carbs 6.2 g; Protein 3.6 g; Fiber 0.4 g

Sweet and Tangy Ketchup

Preparation: 5 minutes   **Cooking: 15 minutes**   **Servings: 2½ cups**

INGREDIENTS

- 1 cup water
- ¼ cup agave syrup
- 1 cup tomato paste
- 3 tbsp apple cider vinegar
- 1 tsp onion powder
- 1 tsp garlic powder

DIRECTIONS

1. Add the water to a medium saucepan and bring to a rolling boil over high heat.
2. Reduce the heat to low, and stitir in the agave syrup, tomato paste, vinegar, onion powder and garlic powder. Cover and bring to a gentle simmer for about 10 minutes, stirring frequently, or until the sauce begins to thicken and bubble.
3. Let the sauce rest for 30 minutes until cooled completely. Transfer to an airtight container and refrigerate for up to 1 month.

Nutritional Facts: Calories 46; Fat 5.2 g; Carbs 1.0 g; Protein 1.1 g; Fiber 1.0 g

Buffalo Dip

Preparation: 10 minutes   **Cooking: 0 minutes**   **Servings: 8**

INGREDIENTS

- 1 cup cauliflower, shredded
- 1 (8-oz.) coconut cream
- ½ cup vegan ranch
- ½ cup cayenne pepper hot sauce
- ½ cup vegan cheese, shredded

DIRECTIONS

1. Add coconut cream and ranch, hot sauce and cheese to a blender.
2. Puree the ingredients together until smooth.
3. Stir in shredded cauliflower and mix with a spoon
4. Serve.
5. Serving Suggestion: Serve the dip with crispy nachos.

Variation Tip: Add crushed red pepper on top before serving.

Nutritional Facts: Calories 225; Fat 15 g; Sodium 345 mg; Carbs 2.3 g; Fiber 1.4 g; Protein 3.3 g;

31-DAY MEAL PLAN

Day	Breakfast	Lunch	Dinner	Dessert
1	Hot and Spicy Savory Oats	Mixed Berries Stew	Tomato Basil Spaghetti	Chocolate Pudding
2	Turmeric Tofu Scramble	Brown Rice and Vegetable Stir-Fry	Vegetable Broth Sans Sodium	Strawberry Ice Cream
3	Apple Avocado Toast	Cauliflower and Roasted Potato Soup	Bean and Rice Burritos	Chia Raspberry Pudding
4	Oatmeal-Raisin Breakfast Bowl	Quinoa and Rice Stuffed Peppers (oven-baked)	Coconut and Grilled Vegetable Soup	Orange Resolution Smoothie
5	Pineapple and Mango Oatmeal	Easy Vegan Pizza Bread	Pesto Quinoa with White Beans	Mango and Cucumber Smoothie
6	Southwestern Tofu Scramble	Wild Rice Mushroom Soup	Raspberry Chia Pudding Shots	Lime and Watermelon Granita
7	Broccoli Puree	Mango and Papaya After-Chop	Tofu Goulash Soup	Melon, Kale, and Broccoli Smoothie
8	Vegan Onion Rings	3-Color Pasta	Roasted Almonds	Cherry-Vanilla Rice Pudding
9	Korean Braised Tofu	Taco Pita Pizzas	Baked Mac and Peas	Beet and Berry Smoothie
10	Lebanese Potato Salad	Sweet Potato Gnocchi	Spinach Chips	Cocoa Cashew Truffles
11	Golden Porridge	Cinnamon Chickpea Energy Bites	One Pan Spicy Rice	Cucumber, Celery, and Apple Smoothie
12	Lemony Millet and Fruit Salad	Pizza Crust	Savory Seed Crackers	Orange-Cranberry Quinoa Bites
13	Banana–Nut Butter Boats	Almond Butter Brownies	Forest Mushroom Loaf	Vegan Chocolate Ice Cream
14	Cinnamon Carrots	Moist Banana Bread	Tomato and Pesto Toast	Kale and Peanut Butter Smoothie
15	Easy Portobello Mushrooms	Peanut Butter–Mocha Energy Bites	Delicious vegan Cheese Bread	Exotic Cream Pie
16	Southwestern Tofu Scramble	Strawberry Bread	Spinach and Dill Pasta Salad	Spicy Carrot, Avocado, and Tomato Smoothie
17	Fruity Yogurt Parfait	Avocado and Sprout Toast	Red Lentil Soup	Chocolate Mousse

18	Macro Miso Breakfast Soup	Wild Rice Mushroom Soup	Chickpea Pecan Salad	Mango Passion Fruit Ice cream
19	Indian-Style Lentil and Potato Hash	Endive and Green Lentil Salad	Cauliflower and Roasted Potato Soup	Almond date and apricot energy bites
20	Morning Muesli	Coconut and Grilled Vegetable Soup	Paprika Sweet Potato	Chocolate Peanut Butter Crispy Bars
21	Jackfruit Louie Avocado Salad	Italian Veggie Salad	Vegetable Broth Sans Sodium	Chocolate Macaroons
22	Artichoke Tofu Salad	Tofu Goulash Soup	Zucchini Stuffed with Mushrooms and Chickpeas	Chocolate Banana Ice Cream
23	Classic Wedge Salad	Potato in Creamy Avocado Salad	Broccoli Fennel Soup	Kale and Peanut Butter Smoothie
24	Hot and Spicy Savory Oats	Mixed Berries Stew	Fresh Citrus Salad with Oranges and Grapefruit	Chocolate Peanut Butter Crispy Bars
25	Indian-Inspired Tofu Scramble	Rice, Chickpea, Fennel, and Orange Salad	Pesto Pea Soup	Cucumber, Celery, and Apple Smoothie
26	Apple Avocado Toast	Chickpea and Spinach Salad	Crusty Grilled Corn on the Cob	Melon, Kale, and Broccoli Smoothie
27	Oatmeal-Raisin Breakfast Bowl	Apple and Hummus Toast	Balsamic Zucchini Bowls	Mango and Cucumber Smoothie
28	Pineapple and Mango Oatmeal	Banana–Chocolate Chip Muffins	Grilled Herb Carrots with Creamy Chickpea Salad	Spicy Carrot, Avocado, and Tomato Smoothie
29	Southwestern Tofu Scramble	Taco Tempeh Salad	Oatmeal Cookies	Orange Resolution Smoothie
30	Korean Braised Tofu	Oven Potato Fries	The Waldorf Salad	Strawberry Ice Cream
31	Lebanese Potato Salad	Mushrooms with Herbs and White Wine	Spaghetti Squash and Leeks	Vegan Chocolate Ice Cream

CONCLUSION

Thank you for reading this book. Now you have everything you need to get started making budget-friendly, healthy plant-based recipes. It's easy to switch over to a plant-based diet if you have your meals planned out and temptation locked away. Don't forget to clean out your kitchen before starting, and you will be sure to meet all your diet and health goals.

I hope that you have enjoyed reading this book as it can help you understand how revolutionary a plant-based diet can be. The information you have learned will help you to make informed decisions as you move toward greater change for the greater good.

When switching to a whole-food, plant-based eating plan, several advantages spring to mind. While these advantages are not instantaneous, they do appear in a reasonably short period. As a result, patience is essential for getting the most out of this new nutritional strategy.

Creating a realistic plan will help you move seamlessly into a whole-food, plant-based diet. You will also require your surroundings to support and focus on your diet plan while doing so. Focus your efforts on studying more about this diet. For example, you can subscribe to YouTube channels to watch and appreciate the videos of other vegans as they share their experiences.

With the recipes in this book, as well as the recommendations I've included, I hope you'll find the whole-food, plant-based diet simple to follow. However, you won't attain your goals unless you have a strong dedication to them.

If your diet becomes monotonous, there is always something fresh to try! The earth is teeming with whole foods that you may experiment with. It would be best if you never were afraid of the unknown. Give everything a go and you'll be on your way to creating your ideal diet in no time.

May you have a healthy and happy life as you believe in yourself and make healthy decisions that serve you in being your best self!

I wish you good luck with a wholefood plant-based diet!

REFERENCES

Appleby PN, Davey GK, Key TJ. Hypertension and blood pressure among meat eaters, fish eaters, vegetarians and vegans in EPIC-Oxford. *Public Health Nutr.* 2002 Oct;5(5):645–54. doi: 10.1079/PHN2002332

Afton Halloran, Holly Rippin, Kremlin Wickramasinghe and Clare Amanda Barrell, 2021, https://www.medicalnewstoday.com/articles/326167

Braun, L and Cohen, M; Herbs & Natural Supplements, an evidence based guide, 2nd Edition, Elsevier, 2007, Iron Monograph (pages 434-442)

Davis BC, Kris-Etherton PM. Achieving optimal essential fatty acid status in vegetarians: current knowledge and practical implications. *Am J Clin Nutr.* 2003 Sep;78(3 Suppl):640S–646S.

El-Sheekh, M.M., Nassef, M., Bases, E. *et al.* Antitumor immunity and therapeutic properties of marine seaweeds-derived extracts in the treatment of cancer. *Cancer Cell Int* 22, 267 (2022). https://doi.org/10.1186/s12935-022-02683-y

Farrand,World Health Organization (Regional Office for Europe) Plant-based diets and their impact on health, sustainability and the environment

Gibbs J, Gaskin E, Ji C, Miller MA and Cappuccio FP. The effect of plant-based dietary patterns on blood pressure: a systematic review and meta-analysis of controlled intervention trials. *Journal of Hypertension*, 2020

Greger Michael M.D. FACLM · Daily Source of Vitamin B12, February 8, 2012 · Volume 7

J Geriatr Cardiol. 2017 May; A plant-based diet for overweight and obesity prevention and treatment, National Library of Medicine14(5): 369–374.doi: 10.11909/j.issn.1671-5411.2017.05.002

Key TJ, Appleby PN, Bradbury KE, Sweeting M, Wood A, Johansson I et al. Consumption of meat, fish, dairy products, and eggs and risk of ischemic heart disease. Circulation. 2019;139(25):2835– 45. doi:10.1161/CIRCULATIONAHA

Marlow HJ, Hayes **WK,Soret S, Carter RL, Schwab ER, Sabaté J**. Diet and the environment: does what you eat matter?*Am J Clin Nutr* 2009;89(suppl):1699S–703S

Melina V, Craig W, Levin S. Position of the Academy of Nutrition and Dietetics: Vegetarian Diets. J Acad Nutr Diet. 2016 Dec;116(12):1970-1980. doi: 10.1016/j.jand.2016.09.025. PMID: 27886704.

N E Allen, T J Key,The effects of diet on circulating sex hormone levels in men, 2000, Dec;13(2):159-84.Nutr Res Rev NIH National Library of Medicine (2017), https://www.ncbi.nlm.nih.gov/pmc/articles/PMC5293796/

NHMRC (National Health and Medical Research Council), Nutrient Reference Values for Australia and New Zealand, Iron, 2005.

Pérez-Jiménez J, Neveu V, Vos F, Scalber A. Identification of the 100 richest dietary sources of polyphenols: an application of the Phenol-Explorer database. *Eur J Clin Nutr.* (2010) 64:S112–20. 10.1038/ejcn.2010.221

Rick Ansorge, Plant-Based Diet for Heart Health Medically Reviewed by James Beckerman, MD, FACC on June 17, 2020. https://www.webmd.com/heart-disease/plant-based-diet-for-heart-health#:~:text=A%20plant%2Dbased%20diet%20can,includes%20a%20lot%20more%20meat

Schepers J, Annemans L. The potential health and economic effects of plant-based food patterns in Belgium and the United Kingdom. Nutrition. 2018;48:24–32. doi:10.1016/j.nut.2017.11.028.

The American Journal of Clinical Nutrition (October, 2019), https://academic.oup.com/ajcn/article/110/4/912/5543218

The American Journal of Clinical Nutrition, Volume 89, Issue 5, May 2009, Pages 1627S–1633S, https://doi.org/10.3945/ajcn.2009.26736N, 2009

Tucker KL, Rich S, Rosenberg I, Jacques P, Dallal G, Wilson PW, et al. Plasma vitamin B-12 concentrations relate to intake source in the Framingham Offspring study. Am J Clin Nutr. (2000) 71:514–22. doi: 10.1093/ajcn/71.2.514 Vafadar,

A., Shabaninejad, Z., Movahedpour, A. et al. Quercetin and cancer: new insights into its therapeutic effects on ovarian cancer cells. Cell Biosci 10, 32 (2020). https://doi.org/10.1186/s13578-020-00397-0

Yaffe-Bellany, David (14 October 2019). "The New Makers of Plant-Based Meat? Big Meat Companies". The New York Times. ISSN 0362-4331.

Williams, Howard. The Ethics of Diet: A Catena of Authorities Deprecatory of the Practice of Flesh Eating. Czechia, Good Press, 2019. https://www.hsph.harvard.edu/nutritionsource/what-should-you-eat/fats-and-cholesterol/types-of-fat/omega-3-fats/#1

Made in the USA
Las Vegas, NV
01 July 2024

91756792R00066